AESTHETICS AND NATURE

Continuum Aesthetics

Series Editor: Derek Matravers, Open University and University of Cambridge, UK

The Continuum Aesthetics Series looks at the aesthetic questions and issues raised by all major art forms. Stimulating, engaging and accessible, the series offers food for thought not only for students of aesthetics, but also for anyone with an interest in philosophy and the arts.

Titles available from Continuum:
Aesthetics and Architecture, Edward Winters
Aesthetics and Literature, David Davies
Aesthetics and Morality, Elisabeth Schellekens
Aesthetics and Music, Andy Hamilton

Forthcoming in 2008:
Aesthetics and Film, Katherine Thomson-Jones
Aesthetics and Painting, Jason Gaiger
Aesthetics and Nature, Glenn Parsons

AESTHETICS AND NATURE

GLENN PARSONS

continuum

Continuum International Publishing Group

The Tower Building	80 Maiden Lane
11 York Road	Suite 704
London SE1 7NX	New York NY 10038

www.continuumbooks.com

© Glenn Parsons, 2008

British Library Cataloguing-in-Publication Data
A catalogue record for this book is available from the British Library.

ISBN-10: HB: 0-8264-9675-X
PB: 0-8264-9676-8
ISBN-13: HB: 978-0-8264-9675-1
PB: 978-0-8264-9676-8

Library of Congress Cataloguing-in-Publication Data

Parsons, Glenn.
Aesthetics and nature/Glenn Parsons.
p. cm.
Includes bibliographical references (p. 153).
ISBN 978-0-8264-9675-1
ISBN 978-0-8264-9676-8
1. Nature (Aesthetics) I. Title.

BH301.N3P37 2008
111′.85—dc22   2008004390

Typeset by Newgen Imaging Systems Pvt Ltd, Chennai, India
Printed and bound in Great Britain by MPG Books Ltd, Bodmin, Cornwall

For Alice

CONTENTS

CONTENTS

INTRODUCTION

Human beings and the natural world have a complicated relationship. Often, and necessarily to some extent, we treat nature as a source of resources for human consumption, and, as such, a commodity that can be bought and sold. At other times, we approach nature with the aim of understanding it, with the perspective of the scientist or natural historian. Sometimes we simply enjoy being in nature, engaging in activities such as snorkelling or hiking. Some see nature through the prism of religion and spirituality, whether an established religious code or more personal beliefs and attitudes. And sometimes, we relate to nature by appreciating its beauty, as when we marvel at the sight of a mighty mountain peak, or gaze with pleasure on a heron labouring in flight. Because human interests and aims are so varied, and because nature itself is so vast, our relationship with the natural world is a many-faceted one. Further, a particular encounter with nature may involve several of these ways of relating to nature, perhaps even concurrently.

The complexity of our relationship to nature can make assessing it a daunting task. But in recent times, the environmental movement has imparted a certain urgency to just this idea. It has become clear that some aspects of our relationship to nature pose significant problems for nature and for us. Consequently, it is incumbent upon us to reflect on the ways that we relate to nature, as complex and multifarious as these are, and to ask what exactly each involves. This book is an introduction to some recent reflection on one of these dimensions of the human–nature relationship: the appreciation of natural beauty. Its aim is to determine more precisely what is involved in the appreciation of natural beauty, and to ask whether it is, ultimately, a worthwhile or acceptable way of relating to nature.

The study of natural beauty can be carried out, of course, in different ways, and many different disciplines have contributed to it. History, geography, sociology and psychology have each delivered valuable insights about natural beauty and our experience of it. This book, however, will generally restrict itself to one particular approach to the subject, that of philosophy, and, more specifically, analytic philosophy. For various reasons, philosophers in the analytic tradition have, historically speaking, neglected natural beauty. But, in the past 30 years, they have taken up this topic, debating natural beauty's nature and significance. The purpose of this book is to introduce you to this work.

As such, the focus of this book is squarely on recent philosophy. A book that traced philosophical views on natural beauty throughout all, or part, of the Western philosophical tradition would be illuminating, but such a book would perhaps require a different focus; it would definitely need a different author. Also, in documenting recent debate, I have chosen not to present the positions of individual thinkers in full detail, but to present more generic positions that amalgamate arguments, distinctions, examples and insights made by various different philosophers. I hope that these generic positions will be more useful in mapping the logical terrain of the field than fully detailed presentations of the views of specific thinkers would be. Readers wanting to explore the views of specific philosophers more fully should find sufficient references cited in the footnotes (for an exhaustive bibliography of the subject, the reader is referred to the introductory essay of *The Aesthetics of Natural Environments*, A. Carlson and A. Berleant (eds), Broadview Press, 2004).

The plan of this book is as follows. Chapters 1 and 2 set the stage for our discussion by introducing the concept of natural beauty and laying out a general approach to understanding it, drawing on some approaches common in analytic philosophy. Chapters 3 through 6 present the positions on appreciating natural beauty that have figured most prominently in recent philosophical debates, along with the principal arguments for and against each. In these chapters, the focus is upon how nature ought to be appreciated aesthetically. In the remaining chapters, the focus shifts to a different, though related, set of issues involving aesthetics and nature. Chapter 7 takes up and critically evaluates an issue that runs throughout the proceeding chapters: the possibility of arguing for the preservation of nature based on its aesthetic value. Finally, in Chapters 8 and 9, I examine the interesting relationship between the aesthetic appreciation of nature and the aesthetic appreciation of two ostensibly related entities: gardens and environmental artworks.

Some of the material in Chapter 9 was presented at the 2007 meeting of the Pacific Division of the American Society for Aesthetics; special thanks to Donald Crawford, Jason Simus, Allen Carlson and Ned Hettinger for helpful discussions. I'm grateful to Yuriko Saito and Allen Carlson for comments on a draft of the book. Thanks also to Derek Matravers, Sarah Campbell and Tom Crick for helping bring it to press, and to Melanie Merglesky for assistance with the index.

CHAPTER I

APPROACHING THE PHILOSOPHY OF NATURAL BEAUTY

In this chapter and the next, we will try to bring our topic into clearer focus. What exactly is natural beauty, and how do we study it philosophically? To flesh out the concept of natural beauty, we will begin by discussing some sceptical attitudes towards it. On these views, natural beauty is a confused idea, and the study of it a waste of time. Although we will ultimately reject these attitudes, considering them will help to clarify the scope and meaning of the concept. We will also look briefly into the history of the concept of natural beauty, to see why many contemporary philosophers prefer to employ a somewhat different concept, that of 'nature's aesthetic qualities'. Finally, we will sketch the particular way in which philosophers go about trying to understand this concept, and offer a basic philosophical definition of it that will be useful in considering different views on the aesthetics of nature.

TWO WORRIES ABOUT NATURAL BEAUTY

In describing the subject matter of this book, the logical place to begin is with the concept of natural beauty. When we bring up our topic, this is the phrase that most readily comes to our lips as a means of characterizing, in a general way, the sort of experiences that we want to consider. We find the phrase sprinkled liberally, for example, throughout tourist ads that describe alluring getaways from the hustle and bustle of cities and urban life. In the United Kingdom, the government has even used this phrase as its official designation for certain scenic sites, such as the Wye Valley, branding them 'Areas of Outstanding Natural Beauty'.[1] However, as useful and intuitive as it is, the concept of natural beauty is not as simple as it appears, and closer scrutiny of it has led some to view the concept with deep suspicion. A consideration of two of these suspicions will help us to clarify the concept, and hence get a better idea of just what our subject matter is.

The first concern arises from the first part of the concept of natural beauty: the concept of nature. The word 'nature' in English is very commonly used to contrast human civilization with the uninhabited regions of the Earth. This sense of the term underlies the idea of nature as a pristine refuge, and our talk of 'escaping' from the city or town and 'getting back to nature'. In this sense of the word, 'nature' means something like 'a place unmodified by humanity'. The idea of such a place is deeply rooted in Western culture, extending back to the Biblical depiction of the Garden of Eden as an untainted paradise. Understood in this way, however, the concept of nature has been subjected to a good deal of criticism. For one thing, critics point out, the extension of the effects of human civilization (e.g. pollution), if not of human civilization itself, has long since extinguished nature, in this sense. There simply is no place left on the planet that is unmodified by humanity. Even in the most remote wilderness area, we can see and perhaps hear traces of humanity's presence, such as the movements of aircraft and satellites overhead, and we can often detect the effects of pollution around us.[2] Given this, there simply is no nature left, and therefore there can be no natural beauty left either.

It may be true that there is no place left on the planet that is untouched by humanity. However, abandoning the concept of nature would clearly be an overreaction to this state of affairs. It would be an overreaction because the criticisms mentioned above are directed at one particular meaning of the word 'nature': place unmodified by humanity. Even if this meaning is now useless, denoting nothing real, as critics hold, 'nature' has other meanings that are worth preserving. For instance, 'nature' is sometimes used with a narrower meaning, to refer to, as John Stuart Mill put it, 'what takes place without the agency, or without the voluntary and intentional agency, of man'.[3] In this sense, an automobile, a black cloud emanating from a smokestack and the arrangement of plants in a garden are all non-natural, since each has come about through the voluntary and intentional agency of human beings. But the clouds in the sky, the motion of the seas and a population of herons could be natural, on this definition, since such things typically do not come about through the voluntary and intentional agency of human beings. Notice that Mill actually offers two definitions, the first more general than, and inclusive of, the second. The former idea of nature – what happens without the agency of man – allows us to exclude from nature events that are brought about by human activity, albeit inadvertently rather than intentionally. On this more general definition, environmental damage from nuclear accidents and storms caused by global warming would be unnatural.[4] The salient point for our purposes here is that even in Mill's more general sense of 'nature', there is plenty of nature left. Even though many things happen because of our presence, many things do not. In fact, it hardly seems possible for humans to destroy nature, in Mill's sense.[5] Further, not all of nature, in this sense, is remote from human beings. Natural things, such as insects and plants, and natural events, such as the fall of rain and the mating behaviours of birds, are all around us, even in the midst of civilization's great cities.

Mill's conception of nature is also frequently criticized, however. Here the charge is that it draws an arbitrary distinction between nature and the human world. It seems that the sciences, and in particular the sciences of evolutionary biology and ecology, have taught us that humans, and by extension human activities, are a part of natural world, not something separate from it. This line of thought holds that, since human civilization arose out of the same physical process that produced forests, birds and orangutans – evolution – it is arbitrary to single out the human world as categorically different from these other things, and from the physical world that produced them. This, however, is precisely the effect of the notion of nature as that which takes place without the agency of human beings. This criticism is more radical than the criticism of the concept of nature as a place unmodified by humanity; this criticism asserts that the concept of nature is not just out of date, like the notion of the typewriter or the beaver pelt hat, but mythological, like the notion of the Olympian gods. For not only is there no longer any nature, as there are no longer typewriters or beaver pelt hats, there never really was any nature in the first place, just as there never was any such being as Zeus or Apollo. What we want to call 'natural processes', such as temperature cycles, animal migration patterns, the behaviour of ocean currents, and so forth, are not fundamentally different from human activities. These sorts of criticisms push us, once again, towards the conclusion that the concept of nature ought to be abandoned as a useless, and actually misleading way of thinking about the world and our place in it. If we accept this conclusion and give up on the term 'nature', then we must, of course, also give up on the term 'natural beauty'.

Abandoning the concept of nature, however, would be a very unfortunate move, because doing so would rob us of an extremely useful concept. It may well be the case that human activities and what we normally call 'natural processes', such as temperature cycles, animal migration patterns, the behaviour of ocean currents, and so forth, ultimately arise from the same source, and have many features in common. But even if this is so, we still often want, and need, to talk generally about the former as opposed to the latter. For instance, we will still want, and need, to worry about how human activities, such as fossil fuel use, are impacting things like temperature cycles, animal migration patterns and the behaviour of ocean currents. But if we throw out the concept 'natural', we are left with no general way to refer to these processes. And in the context of discussing beauty, we will still want, and need, to talk about the beauty of birds, mountains, oceans and starry skies as opposed to the beauty of cathedrals and paintings. But if we simply jettison the concept of nature, we are left without any general way to refer to these things. The wholesale rejection of the concept of nature would thus unnecessarily hamper the study of beauty. In our discussion, therefore, we will continue to employ the term 'nature' to refer to that which takes place without the agency of human beings.[6]

In addition to concerns about the notion of natural beauty that are raised in relation to the concept of nature, another worry emerges from the notion's other component: the concept of beauty. As with the concept of nature, the basic concern is that the concept of beauty is, if not empty, at least misleading. We can consider two forms of this concern here. The first turns on the observation that the word 'beautiful' seems to be, as the nineteenth-century British philosopher Richard Payne Knight put it, 'applied indiscriminately to almost every thing that is pleasing'.[7] A fine shot in tennis, a clever stock trade, a mathematical theorem, a good crop of tomatoes and a prize bass can all be referred to in English, without strain, as 'beautiful', or more colloquially, as 'real beauties'. Since it seems that these various things have little in common, to call them beautiful appears to be nothing more than a fancy way of saying that each is good, or excellent. As Knight nicely summed it up, 'the word Beauty is a general term of approbation, of the most vague and extensive meaning'.[8] If this is correct, then the study of the beauty of nature is, really, just the study of the excellence or goodness of nature. But if so, the word 'beauty' is simply otiose. Rather than confuse matters, it would be clearer to leave it behind and talk plainly about the goodness or excellence of things in nature.

A second sort of worry about the concept of beauty is based on the fact that, at least in some cases, the word 'beauty' is used primarily as a means of conveying feelings of tenderness and affection. When a husband rises at his fifteenth wedding anniversary to pay tribute to his 'beautiful wife', for instance, we don't take him to imply that she ought to take up modelling. What he means to convey in calling her 'beautiful' is the extent of the love he feels for her, or the qualities of her character that inspire that love. To take another case, it is a piece of received wisdom that a baby, regardless of its looks, is beautiful to its parents. This insight is readily explained by the fact that, in calling their child beautiful, what parents are really doing is not so much commenting on its looks as expressing their love for it. What these instances suggest is that the word 'beauty' is often a slightly indirect means of expressing feelings of love or moral regard. This use of 'beauty' is particularly salient for the case of nature, since many people have strong feelings of love and attachment to certain natural places and things. The philosopher R.G. Collingwood noted that 'the bright eyes of a mouse or the fragile vitality of a flower are things that touch us to the heart . . . with the love that life feels for life'.[9] As such, we are tempted to describe these things as beautiful, in much the way that parental love naturally impels every father to declare his child beautiful, whatever he or she looks like. But this raises the worry that, in talking about natural beauty, what we are really doing is talking about something else – namely our love of nature – in an indirect and needlessly confusing way. Again, the term 'beauty' does not really add anything useful to the discussion, but only obscures the true nature of what we are discussing. This being the case, principles of clarity and forthrightness mandate that we would be better off junking the phrase altogether.

What can we say in response to these criticisms of 'beauty'? As in the case of nature, the points made about the use of the word 'beauty' seem accurate. 'Beauty' *is* often used simply to indicate goodness or excellence, and it is also often used to express love or moral regard.[10] Tolstoy once called beauty 'the all-confusing concept', and he was on to something, since like the term 'nature', 'beauty' has a number of different meanings that are easily confused.[11] However, also as in the case of nature, the fact that some of these meanings are misleading, and so not useful, does not mean that all of them are. In addition to the meanings mentioned above, there is also a narrower sense of 'beauty', on which the term refers to the perceptual appearances of things, and especially to a way, or a range of ways, that they look or sound. Taken this way, to say that something is 'beautiful' is not merely to say that it is excellent, nor just to express one's love for it; rather it is to point out that it has a particular kind of perceptual appearance – for instance, a particular kind of look or sound. That there is beauty, in this sense, is proved by the fact that we occasionally call odious and mediocre people, some celebrities, for instance, beautiful. Though they lack any sort of excellence, and make no claim on our love or affection, we have to admit that the way they look is an instance of that particular kind of sensory appearance that we call 'beauty'.

The lesson to draw from these criticisms of the concept of natural beauty is that, although 'natural beauty' is a nebulous and ambiguous phrase, and even though some of the ways in which it is used can be confusing and misleading, it can be useful as a way of referring to an important concept, so long as we are careful to assign a specific meaning to it. Putting together the senses of 'natural' and 'beauty' that we have isolated above, we can assign 'natural beauty' the following specific meaning: a certain kind of perceptual appearance possessed by what takes place or comes into being without the agency of human beings. This seems to capture more or less what tourist ads aim to convey in flogging the natural beauty of their exotic getaways, and what the British government is trying to preserve when it confers legal protection on its Areas of Outstanding Natural Beauty. As such, this definition of 'natural beauty' gives us a useful starting point for our discussion.

I say 'a starting point' because, although it is natural to begin any discussion of this topic with the concept of natural beauty, most contemporary philosophers are actually rather reluctant to use the term 'beauty'. They prefer to speak instead of the 'aesthetic qualities' of natural things. This may seem like a verbal quibble, but the preference has an important purpose. To understand it, we need to undertake a brief digression into the history of taste for nature in the Western world.

A SHORT HISTORY OF TASTE IN LANDSCAPE

Given the way that we have defined it, the notion of natural beauty probably seems quite obvious and unremarkable to you. That is, the fact that some natural things have the particular sort of sensory appearance that can be described as 'beautiful' is not news. One only needs to look at natural areas such as the Rocky Mountains, or some of Britain's Areas of Outstanding Natural Beauty, or at magnificent animals such as the lion and the polar bear, to see that this is true. Indeed, at least in Western culture, these natural things have become paradigms of beauty: they are the sort of basic examples that we use in teaching the meaning of the word 'beautiful' to children or to people trying to learn the English language.[12] It is true that the concept of natural beauty can seem a bit hazy around the edges – it may not be clear to you whether certain natural things are beautiful or not. And some cases are disputed: you may think that cobras are beautiful, while others may disagree. Nonetheless, it is probably true that every person can think of a particular clear example of a natural thing that she would describe, unhesitatingly, with the word 'beautiful'. In this sense, the idea that beauty can exist in nature is not an obscure or problematic one: on the contrary it seems obvious, a matter of common sense. But this was not always the case. Prior to the eighteenth century, it was rarer, and more difficult, to think of nature as beautiful, and the idea that nature could be a paradigm of beauty would probably have seemed alien.

Three reasons for this peculiarity in the history of taste are worth considering here. The first relates to the way in which beauty had been conceived in the great civilizations of antiquity, Greece and Rome. The terms corresponding to the English word 'beautiful' in the classical languages, *kalon* in Greek and *pulchrum* in Latin, were often understood in terms of mathematical properties, especially the concept of proportion. In its most general sense, proportion refers to the size, number and arrangement of the parts in a complex whole.[13] When applied to objects of sensory perception, the conception of beauty as proportion produced the idea that a beautiful object is one that embodies qualities such as symmetry, balance and harmony among its constituent parts. This conception of the beautiful shows up in philosophical works such as Plato's *Philebus*, wherein we read that 'measure and proportion manifest themselves in all areas as beauty and virtue'.[14] And, of course, we see it manifested in the great works of classical sculpture and architecture, such as the Parthenon. The stately, refined look characteristic of sound proportion is what we refer to today when we say that a building or a statue has a 'classical' appearance.

The classical conception of beauty as 'just proportion' remained the dominant way of thinking about beauty in the West from antiquity up until the eighteenth century. The historian of aesthetics Wladyslaw Tatarkiewicz went so far as to call this idea 'The Great Theory of Beauty', saying that 'there have been few theories in any branch of European culture which have endured so long or commanded such widespread recognition'.[15] The significance of this view for the history of natural beauty is that, while it applied easily to the human world, it was more difficult to apply to nature. For the ancients the human form itself was a paradigm of symmetry and proportion, the same qualities found in well-made buildings.[16] But in the natural amalgamations of stone, water and wood that compose the landscape, irregularity, rather than proportion, is the rule. In nature, for instance, even as basic a regular form as the right ple is almost completely absent.[17] The upshot of this is that, for most the history of the West, natural beauty was not an obvious bit of common sense, but something of an oxymoron. To the extent that the landscape was beautiful, it was because human forces had imbued it with proportion, as when trees, flowers and hedges were carefully composed to produce a formal garden.[18]

A second important factor that long stymied appreciation of natural beauty in the West was the fact that, prior to the late seventeenth century, people in the West had relatively little opportunity to appreciate the way nature looked. The sort of scenic nature tourism, or 'sightseeing', that is so prevalent in today's culture was largely an innovation of the eighteenth century. Prior to this time, travel to the wilder regions of Europe, when not precluded altogether by war, was inconvenient and, frequently, downright dangerous. A crossing of the Alps, for instance, was fraught with the dangers of wild animals, inadequate roads and periodic banditry. The intrepid travellers who were undeterred by these factors seem to have generally left the Alpine regions with a predominant feeling of relief, rather than admiration for what they had seen.[19]

A third factor that was historically important in hampering the appreciation of natural beauty was the influence of particular religious beliefs concerning nature. In Christian thought, for example, one view on the provenance of mountains was that they were not a part of God's original creation.[20] Originally, the world had perfect spherical proportions and hence, according to traditional thought, was beautiful. Mountains came later, being the literal debris of the upheaval associated with the deluge of the Earth described in the Bible. As such, mountains were a visible sign of man's sinfulness and the fallen nature of this world. In this context, the idea of taking mountains to be beautiful probably seemed simply bizarre, if not outright heretical. Together, these three factors – the classical heritage of thinking about beauty, the inaccessibility of natural areas and the influence of certain religious doctrines – made the idea of natural beauty a dubious one in the period before the eighteenth century. They contributed to a cultural climate in which natural things that we would regard as superlatively beautiful – the Alps – were generally despised as 'warts' upon creation, or, as the English diarist John Evelyn put it, 'the rubbish of the Earth'.[21]

In the eighteenth century, however, the importance of these factors began to wane, at least to some extent. The Treaty of Utrecht in 1713 allowed a resumption of the traditional English practice of the Continental tour, wherein young gentlemen would spend a few months absorbing the sights and culture of Europe.[22] The tour started up again and quickly gained in popularity, with the crossing of the Alps becoming a particular highlight of the trip, rather than a mere hardship. The increased contact with Italy brought about by the tour resulted in an infusion of new influences into English landscape painting, as works by European masters such as Salvador Rosa, Claude Lorrain and Gaspar Dughet found their way to England.[23] At around the same time, new trends in natural philosophy, and particularly geology, began to challenge traditional ways of thinking about mountains. Instead of the direct and relatively recent detritus of a supernatural event, mountains came to be understood as important natural phenomena in their own right.[24] As a consequence of these and other factors, the eighteenth-century traveller was prepared to see nature in a fresh light. The result was an unprecedented expansion in the scope of taste, and a movement away from the classical ideal of beauty as regularity and proportion.

This expansion is most clearly evident in the emergence of two new concepts during this period: the picturesque and the sublime. The concept of the picturesque is a difficult one to pin down.[25] We can get a handle on the notion, however, by focusing on its paradigmatic use to refer to landscapes of the particular varieties depicted by early continental landscape painters, such as Rosa, Lorrain and Dughet. These painters focused on pastoral scenes that were characterized by irregular shapes, sudden variations and rough textures.[26] The typical picturesque landscape painting included a body of water, usually of irregular shape, clouds, trees with variegated foliage and other elements such as ruins, winding paths and animals. The works of these painters fed a taste for actual landscapes with these qualities, in contrast to the traditional taste for more regular, cultivated landscapes, such as formal gardens. The picturesque thus laid the foundation for a new approach to landscaping and gardening, and a new way of appreciating the land.

The other key concept to emerge in this period is the concept of the sublime. Whereas the picturesque applied paradigmatically to gently irregular and variegated countrysides, the sublime described nature in its wilder manifestations. The German philosopher Kant described the range of typically sublime scenes as follows:

> Bold, overhanging, as it were threatening cliffs, thunder clouds towering up into the heavens, bringing with them flashes of lightning

and crashes of thunder, volcanoes with their all-destroying violence, hurricanes with the devastation they leave behind, the boundless ocean set into a rage, a lofty waterfall on a mighty river, etc. . . .[27]

The sublime was a radical departure from previous ways of thinking of beauty in nature. Rather than neatly proportioned, the sublime was vast and irregular; rather than a series of gently variegated patterns, it presented violent motion and upheaval. Whereas previous travellers had responded to these elements in the Alps with fear and trepidation, eighteenth-century visitors could now find what John Dennis called 'a delightful horror, a terrible Joy' in them.[28]

Together, the picturesque and the sublime helped to displace the classical concept of beauty from the centre of taste for landscape. Nature might not have a beautiful appearance in the classical sense, but eighteenth-century sensibility discovered that nature possesses other appearances that offer just as much, if not more, to a refined taste. A character in a dialogue by the third Earl of Shaftesbury epitomized the new mood:

I shall no longer resist the passion growing in me for things of a natural kind, where neither art nor the conceit or caprice of man has spoiled their genuine order by breaking in on that primitive state. Even the rude rocks, the mossy caverns, the irregular unwrought grottos and broken falls of waters, with all the horrid graces of the wilderness itself, as representing Nature more, will be the more engaging, and appear with a magnificence beyond the formal mockery of princely gardens . . .[29]

The foregoing digression into historical changes in the taste for landscape allows us to better understand the phenomenon noted at the end of the previous section: contemporary philosophers' tendency to eschew the term 'beauty'. Although the dominance of the classical conception of beauty as proportion has long since ended, the word has retained some of its classical connotations. As the taste in landscape broadened, 'beauty' came to be associated primarily with the older, classical approach. Hence, using the term 'natural beauty' as a general description of the visual appeal of landscape tends to focus attention on those natural things that are more regular and symmetrical, as opposed to those with different sorts of visual appeal, such as picturesque and sublime scenes. For example, it seems very intuitive to describe a maple leaf, symmetrical and regular in its shape, as beautiful, but the label fits less comfortably when applied to an enormous, raging waterfall.

This being the case, many philosophers feel that 'beauty' is no longer an apt term for describing, *in a general way*, the sensory appearances that appeal to our taste in landscape. A better term would apply equally fittingly to the subtle irregularities of shape and colour in the floor of a redwood forest, to the overpowering rush of a waterfall and to the pleasing symmetry of a leaf. For this purpose philosophers now employ the term 'aesthetic quality'. As philosophers use it, this term usually refers to any kind of pleasing visual or auditory appearance, including the splendour of the starry heavens, the exquisite geometry of a leaf's shape and the intricate patterns of a forest floor. The word 'beauty' remains the most intuitive way for most of us to begin talking about our responses to landscape. But in trying to think philosophically about the nature of those responses, the concept of an 'aesthetic quality' will be more useful. Henceforth, then, instead of the beauty of nature, let us take nature's aesthetic qualities to be our subject-matter. When we need to refer, more generally, to the phenomenon of nature possessing aesthetic qualities, or to our appreciation or judgement of these qualities, we will speak simply of 'the aesthetics of nature'.

PHILOSOPHICAL DEFINITION AND 'HAVING AN AESTHETIC QUALITY'

As the previous section's cursory overview will have revealed, the taste for landscape has a most interesting history. In the West, it has undergone extensive change, particularly in the eighteenth century. Since that time, of course, aesthetic taste in landscape has continued to evolve in all sorts of different directions. Also, if we look to different cultures, we find still further differences in the sorts of natural things found aesthetically pleasing. In Japanese culture, for example, we find a special emphasis on natural things that express the qualities of fragility and transience, such as cherry blossoms, bird songs, morning dew and rain.[30] Historians and sociologists have documented many of these differences across time and space, and explained them by uncovering their connections to more general differences in the world-views and attitudes of different cultures and periods. The Japanese interest in natural things that express transience, for instance, has been connected to the Zen Buddhist conception that all things are inherently impermanent. In recent times, even biologists have tried their hand at explaining why we have certain responses to land-scapes, drawing on the idea of natural selection.[31]

These investigations into the aesthetics of nature are interesting and valuable, but they are different in focus from the sort that typically occupies the philosopher. The philosopher's investigation of the aesthetics of nature does not focus on people's conceptions of what nature's aesthetic qualities actually are, nor on how these precise conceptions, rather than others, achieved currency. The philosopher's aim, rather, is to discover what conception of nature's aesthetic qualities we *ought* to hold. The philosopher aims to do this primarily by trying to formulate, in very general terms, what the concept of 'aesthetic quality' means, or, to put it another way, what precisely we are talking about when we talk about the aesthetic qualities of nature. The goal, in other words, is to formulate a *philosophical definition* of what exactly having aesthetic qualities consists in.

What would such a definition look like? A general answer to this question is difficult, since philosophers themselves tend to disagree about what makes for a good philosophical definition. We can get a rough idea, however, by identifying two characteristics of a good philosophical definition. The first of these is capturing the *essence* of the concept. Consider the following definition of the term 'bachelor', for example: a fun-loving and irresponsible person. This is a poor definition of 'bachelor' because, even if many bachelors are fun-loving and irresponsible, these qualities do not constitute the essence of bachelorhood, but only things that sometimes occur along with bachelorhood. Our definition has missed the essence of bachelorhood, or what really makes something a bachelor, and as such it fails to tell us what bachelorhood really *is*. In order for a definition to capture the essence of bachelorhood, it ought to apply to *all* the things that the term applies to, and *only* to things to which the term applies. As philosophers often put it, a philosophical definition of a term must state conditions that are individually necessary and jointly sufficient for the application of that term. Take a better definition of 'bachelor': unmarried male. This definition states two conditions that are jointly sufficient for the application of the term 'bachelor', being unmarried and being male, since if any object satisfies both of these conditions, then 'bachelor' applies to that object. Also, the conditions given by our definition are each of them necessary for the application of the term 'bachelor': if any thing is a bachelor, then it must be unmarried, and it must be male. So being an unmarried male, we might say, *always* produces bachelorhood and, furthermore, is *the only thing* that produces it.

What this means is that our second definition, unlike the lame one offered above, captures the essence of bachelorhood. It does not merely tell us something about bachelorhood (e.g. that it is sometimes associated with irresponsibility): it tells us what bachelorhood, itself, is.

The second feature that philosophers look for in a good philosophical definition is that it break down the concept that we wish to understand into simpler notions, thereby revealing its nature. We can see this in the case of 'bachelor': by breaking the concept down into the simpler concepts *being male* and *being unmarried*, our definition would allow someone unfamiliar with the concept to understand it. For concepts like bachelor, of course, this sort of clarification is easily obtained: one can look in a good dictionary and obtain the relevant understanding. But for the concepts focused on by philosophers – very general and abstract concepts such as truth, justice and knowledge – such clarification is more elusive, and here even the best dictionaries are of little help. To use an example from a different branch of philosophy, one influential philosophical definition of the concept 'ethical action' is 'an action that increases the total sum of human happiness'. By breaking the concept of an ethical action down into simpler concepts like maximization and happiness, this definition is supposed to not only pin down the essence of ethical action, but to lay bare its nature for us. In this fashion, then, good philosophical definitions ought to clarify and illuminate concepts that are initially difficult and obscure.

The two features described above should convey some sense of what a distinctively philosophical study of the aesthetics of nature involves. They also allow us to see how that investigation differs from studies carried out by the historian and the sociologist. For while the historian needs to be able to identify the things that, at a given time, people view as having aesthetic qualities, doing this does not require that she state, or even possess, a set of conditions that are individually necessary and jointly sufficient for the application of the concept 'having an aesthetic quality'. Nor does she need to explain what the concept is, in the sense of breaking it down into simpler notions. To put the point another way, and to slip back into the more old-fashioned language of beauty for a moment, historical accounts tell us what things people have called 'beautiful' over the course of history, and why they did so. But in philosophy we seek, as Socrates once put it, 'not what is beautiful, but what is beauty'.[32]

Sometimes people look askance at the attempt to provide philosophical definitions for concepts such as 'having an aesthetic quality', truth, ethical action, and the like, seeing the attempt to define these very abstract and historically evolving concepts as naïve. Such a sceptic might ask: 'How can one hope to reduce a concept so abstract, complex, and dynamic to a few simple conditions?' The sceptic might also question the need to even attempt this in the first place. Surely, he could say, no one needs a philosophical definition to apply phrases like 'has an aesthetic quality' or 'is an ethical action'. And if we wish to know how we *ought* to understand such concepts, perhaps history will serve as a better guide than philosophy by revealing their origins and the ways in which people have used them, for better or for ill, in the past.

Our hypothetical sceptic would be right on a number of points. He is certainly correct in saying that arriving at philosophical definitions of these concepts is difficult, for philosophy is a difficult enterprise. He is also correct in saying that people do not require a philosophical definition of complex concepts, such as 'ethical action', in order to use those concepts. Most of us confidently aver that enslaving people is not an ethical action, for example, even though we cannot produce a philosophical definition of the concept 'ethical action'. We can do this because, in the course of our experience, we have encountered other people referring to certain actions with the word 'unethical', acts of enslavement among them. From this experience, and our study of the disastrous historical legacy of slavery, we learn to apply the label to similar actions. In this sense, the sceptic is right to say that no one needs a philosophical definition to use concepts like 'ethical action'.

Nonetheless, our sceptic's position is overstated, for there is another sense in which each of us *does* need a philosophical definition of the concepts that we use. When a man says that slavery is unethical, he believes that he is asserting something true: that slavery is unethical. But the mere fact that people before him have applied the words 'unethical' to slavery, in itself, does not justify this belief. After all, people are often mistaken about such matters. Not so long ago, for example, most people were unwilling to apply the term 'unethical' to slavery. When a man says that slavery is unethical, he assumes not just that the phrase 'unethical action' happens to have been associated with slavery in the past, but that it has been *correctly* associated with it. That is, he believes that this phrase has a definite meaning, and on that meaning, whatever it is, it is true that enslavement is an unethical act. He believes this even when, as is typically the case, he has not got that definition of 'ethical action' ready to hand. Most likely he tacitly assumes that someone else has it, or that someone in the past has worked it out, or perhaps that some being, God perhaps, is capable of working it out, such that he need not go through the bother of formulating it for himself. But nonetheless he assumes that such a definition is possible, for if he did not, he would have no reason to believe that what he says about slavery being unethical is *true*. So even though individuals do not need philosophical definitions of complex concepts in order to use them in daily life, such definitions remain necessary as part of the ultimate basis for our beliefs involving those concepts.

The concept of having an aesthetic quality is no exception to this rule, and consequently philosophers have made various attempts to provide a philosophical definition of it. In this book, however, our focus is not the concept of having an aesthetic quality *per se*, but rather aesthetic qualities belonging to nature. Consequently, we will not pursue a complete philosophical definition of 'aesthetic quality'; rather, we will formulate one that, while incomplete, will allow us to bring out those issues of particular interest with respect to nature. Our discussion of beauty and the aesthetic so far already provides us with the basis for such a definition. We have already noted the connection of aesthetic qualities with perception, and in particular sense perception. Aesthetic qualities seem to be a matter primarily of how things look or sound to us. Our previous discussion also hinted that 'aesthetic quality' refers to a particular kind of perceptual appearance: that which produces pleasure or displeasure when we experience it. Recall again our discussion of the emergence of the sublime as a new sort of aesthetic quality in nature. Violent and dishevelled natural objects, such as thunderstorms and great waterfalls, became objects of taste when observers were able to take 'delightful horror, a terrible Joy' in them. It seems that the ability of a sensory appearance to provide delight, joy, or, more generally, pleasure or displeasure to the viewer is an important element in what makes something an aesthetic quality. Based on this line of thought, we can offer the following as a provisional philosophical definition of the concept 'having an aesthetic quality': possessing a pleasing or displeasing perceptual appearance.

This definition needs some refinement, however, before we can be confident that it captures, even in a very rough way, the essence of the concept of having an aesthetic quality. For it seems that the definition is too broad, classifying as aesthetic qualities things that, in actual practice, we would hesitate to label as such. This is so in at least two respects.

In the first place, our definition includes cases where our pleasure seems to come from the wrong source. In the eighteenth century, Shaftesbury noted that the perceptual appearances of things can please us, not because of their appearance *per se*, but because of certain desires that we associate strongly with those appearances. As an example consider a farmer gazing contentedly at her field of corn. She finds its visual appearance pleasing indeed, but not for its own sake: rather, it pleases only because it indicates to her that she will have a rich harvest. In such cases, Shaftesbury argued, 'you will own the enjoyment . . . to be very different from that which should naturally follow from the contemplation of . . . beauty'.[33] This case seems to show that having a pleasing sensory appearance is not sufficient for having an aesthetic quality. What we need to add is an insistence that the pleasure come simply from the experience of perceiving the appearance itself, and not from the satisfaction of our independent, pre-existing desires. To accommodate Shaftesbury's insight, we can revise our philosophical definition of 'aesthetic quality' to read: a perceptual appearance that is pleasing or displeasing *for its own sake.*

Contemporary philosophers sometimes describe the latter feature as 'disinterestedness'. To say that someone is disinterested in something does not mean that she is 'uninterested' in that thing, but only that her interest does not stem from a personal advantage to be gained. Thus, a neutral party called in to solve a dispute should certainly be interested in finding a solution, but she should also be disinterested, in the sense that, in advancing a solution, she puts aside her own aims and desires, focusing only on the interests of the disputants. In an aesthetic context, we are disinterested when we put aside our own practical aims and desires, taking pleasure or displeasure only in the perceptual appearance of the object.

Even after modifying our definition in this way, however, it may still be overly broad. For our definition leaves open the possibility of aesthetic qualities arising in experiences had through the so-called 'proximal senses' of taste, smell and touch. But many philosophers have thought that the pleasures arising from eating, smelling and touching ought to be kept distinct from the aesthetic qualities that we find in sights and sounds.[34] One reason for this view is that a sensory experience's being pleasing or displeasing for its own sake does not seem sufficient to give it aesthetic qualities: the soothing tactile sensations we get when taking a warm bath, or the physical pleasures of sexual intercourse, for instance, are highly pleasant, for their own sake, but we neither describe these as involving aesthetic qualities, nor group them with things that we do enjoy aesthetically, such as artworks. The crucial difference between these cases and cases of pleasure taken in sight and hearing seems to be that the pleasures of the proximal senses are, at least typically, felt as bodily sensations, whereas the pleasures associated with sight and hearing are not. The pleasure that we experience in watching the graceful movements of a gazelle, for example, whatever the precise nature of that pleasure may be, is not directly felt in any particular region of our body. In cases such as the warm bath and sexual intercourse, the pleasure is felt directly in more or less localized regions of the body. The sort of pleasure that we refer to when we say that a thing has an aesthetic quality seems to be the former variety, and not the latter. The pleasure involved in aesthetic qualities, we might say, transcends the body: it is, as it were, disembodied pleasure.[35]

If this line of thought is correct – as we will see in Chapter 6, some philosophers would dispute it – then we ought to narrow our definition of 'aesthetic quality' further, to something like: a visual or auditory appearance that is pleasing or displeasing *for its own sake*. This philosophical definition of 'aesthetic quality' is certainly not the only one that philosophers have given.[36] It is also incomplete, and if we wanted a fully satisfactory definition, a set of conditions that are individually necessary and jointly sufficient, there are a number of issues we would need to address. But this definition has been extremely influential in recent philosophy, and as such it is part of the background against which the important contemporary theories about the aesthetics of nature have taken shape. In the next chapter, we begin to take up those theories, after addressing one further issue for our conception of aesthetic qualities: the role of thinking.

CHAPTER 2

IMAGINATION, BELIEF AND THE AESTHETICS OF NATURE

The philosophical definition of 'aesthetic quality' introduced in the previous chapter can be viewed as involving two main elements. It has, first, a sensory element, since, according to the definition, aesthetic qualities are a matter of the perceptual appearances, in particular the looks or sounds, of things. If a thing is elegant, for example, this means that the particular array of shapes, colours and sounds that it presents to our senses has the capacity to please us, in itself. As we have seen, it is also necessary to introduce a second element, which we might call the 'affective' element, dealing with desires. The affective dimension of our definition rules out cases where we take pleasure in the sensory appearance of a thing because of the satisfaction of some desire, rather than a delight in the sensory appearance *per se*. Together, these elements give us a general conception of what it is for an object to have an aesthetic quality: to be graceful, hideous, sublime, and so forth. In this chapter, to further develop this conception, and as a way of introducing our first account of the aesthetic appreciation of nature, we will add a third element to this conception: thought.

THE ROLE OF THOUGHT

'Thought' is a word that is sometimes used to refer to any sort of thing that can be 'in one's mind': the experience of bodily sensations, such as warmth and pain, the awareness of raw visual and auditory impressions, such as those caused by seeing a certain shade of blue or hearing a particular musical note, emotions like jealousy and joy, beliefs, and much more besides. But here we will use it in a narrower sense, one in which thinking is different from mere experience or awareness. To think, in this sense, is to carry out a mental operation that involves what philosophers call a 'proposition'. Propositions are often described as what is asserted when one makes an assertion. As such, propositions can be described by declarative sentences, and are generally either true or false.[1] The sentence

'It rained in Toronto on 26 May 2007', for example, describes a proposition. When I assert that it rained in Toronto on 26 May 2007, this proposition is what I assert. Further, this proposition is either true or false: either it did rain in Toronto on 26 May 2007, in which case the proposition I assert is true, or it did not, in which case that proposition is false.

We can use the notion of a proposition to introduce the narrower sense of the term 'thought' that we are going to use here in the following way. When we think, we perform certain kinds of mental operations: operations that involve propositions. Thus to believe that it rained yesterday, to hope that it will rain tomorrow, to want it to rain and to imagine it raining, are all forms of thinking in our narrower sense. In essentially involving some relationship to a proposition, they are fundamentally different from other mental activities, such as the mere experiencing of a bodily sensation of warmth or a pain. For in these latter cases, our mental processes do not involve a proposition: bodily sensations of warmth and raw visual impressions of blue are not the sort of thing that one can assert, nor can they be true or false.[2]

At first glance, it might seem that experiencing aesthetic qualities has nothing to do with thinking, but takes place entirely at the level of our mere experience of sensation. When we experience aesthetic qualities, it may be thought, we simply 'take in' the object's raw sensory appearance, and find pleasure, or displeasure, in doing so. It may seem a matter of 'just looking' (or listening) and nothing more, leaving no role for thinking. But although the experiencing of immediate or raw sensations is not itself a form of thought, it is, of course, not incompatible with thinking. Most of the looking and listening that we do involves the experience of sensations in close conjunction with all sorts of thinking. Further, if we reflect on cases of experiencing aesthetic qualities, we find that many of these experiences have what Ronald Hepburn calls a 'thought-component' – a thought sequence that is an integral element of the pleasure we experience.[3] Hepburn gives the example of what he calls 'a paradigm aesthetic experience of nature – the fall of an autumn leaf'. He writes:

If we simply watch it fall, without any thought, it may or may not be a moving or exciting aesthetic object, but it must be robbed of its poignancy, its mute message of summer gone, its symbolizing *all* falling, our own included. Leaf veins suggest blood-vessel veins – symbolizing continuity in the forms of life, and maybe a shared vulnerability. Thus the thought element may bring analogies to bear on the concrete particulars: this autumn is linked to innumerable other autumns: to the cycle of the seasons.[4]

Hepburn's description makes plain how large a role the thought component can play, even in apparently simple experiences of aesthetic qualities. We find the particular perceptual appearance of the falling leaf pleasing here largely because of the thoughts with which we infuse it.

It is important to bear in mind, however, that, when we appreciate aesthetic qualities, what we find pleasing or displeasing is still the perceptual appearance of the object. The thoughts of transience and change that Hepburn describes can also be enjoyed apart from the perceptual experience that we get by watching a falling leaf: we may simply take pleasure in reflecting, abstractly, on these profound ideas. But when we aesthetically appreciate a falling leaf, we are not simply revelling in these ideas: if this were all there was to it, we could have the very same aesthetic experience in a completely leafless environment, such as a submarine or a parking garage. Rather, when we aesthetically appreciate a falling leaf, it is the perceptual appearance in which we delight, albeit fused with, and modified by, these thoughts of transience and change. The leaf's fall pleases because it *looks* poignant, a delicate tremor in nature that is yet pregnant with larger significance. But it looks that way because of the thought component that we bring to our perceptual experience.

If we adopt the view that thought plays a role in our experience of aesthetic qualities, then we must come to view such experience as quite complex. For one thing, we must recognize that there are different types of thought that may be involved. Perhaps the most obvious of these is belief. In the example of the falling leaf, for example, part of the thought component is the belief that every living thing, like the leaf, must necessarily pass away. But other aspects of the thought component need not be beliefs: imagination, for example, can also play a role.[5] We may imagine the leaf veins as blood vessels, as Hepburn suggests, or we may imagine ourselves falling into oblivion, in the way the leaf does. In imagining the leaf veins as blood vessels, our mental activity involves a proposition (these are blood vessels). But we relate to the proposition in a somewhat different way than we do in belief. To use some metaphors, we might say that when we imagine, we 'hold the proposition up in front of our minds' instead of truly 'embracing it', as we do in belief. If one believed, rather than merely imagined, that the leaf veins were full of blood, one would no doubt respond quite differently (for one would then see them as part of a bizarre, if not grotesque, organism). But insofar as imagination and belief each involve relating to a proposition, we group them together as forms of thought.

Even greater complexity emerges when we consider the possible sources for thoughts to bring to our aesthetic experiences of nature. One obvious source is natural science, one main aim of which, after all, is to tell us things about the composition and behaviour of natural things. Sciences such as geology, biology and natural history provide us with a rich source of thought about the natural world that we might bring to our aesthetic experience of it. In the leaf example, for instance, we might expand our thought content to include the fact that the colour changes in autumn leaves are not really cases of leaves gaining new colour, but of pigments already present in the leaves being unmasked by the depletion of chlorophyll. This might change, again, our response to the look of autumn forests. Instead of seeing them as bearing the mute message of 'summer gone', we might see them as bearing the mute message of 'nature purified'.

Science is by no means the only source of thoughts about nature, however. Another rich source is history. When we view a natural area or landscape we may imagine past events and long gone inhabitants. This sort of appreciation of landscape is characteristic of Asian and European attitudes to landscape, given the long and rich cultural history of those continents, but is also found in more recently settled areas of Australia and the Americas. In North America, battlefields, such as those at Gettysburg, Pennsylvania and the Plains of Abraham in Quebec, are popular tourist attractions where visitors are encouraged to imagine past armies charging over the surrounding terrain. The history of indigenous peoples plays a similar role in stimulating, and enriching, appreciation of the landscape. Janna Thompson offers the example of the Merri Creek grassland in South Australia. The fact that this is one of the last instances of native grassland as it existed before the arrival of white settlers, and a traditional home for the indigenous Koori people, Thompson claims, gives our experience of it 'resonance and depth'.[6]

Leaving the factual domains of science and history, we can identify a number of other sorts of narrative that we may draw on for the thought component of our aesthetic appreciation of nature, such as cultural myths and legends, as well as the narratives of the various religious traditions. These accounts assign meaning and significance to various natural phenomena. The ancient Greeks took lightning to be the wrath of Zeus and the constellations the product of various transformations brought about by the gods. These stories can infuse our perceptual experience of nature, whether we believe in them, as the ancient Greeks did, or whether we simply imagine the events that they describe. It was this sort of richer encounter with nature, as a setting for the fantastic events of legend, that Wordsworth celebrated in his famous lines:

> I'd rather be
> A Pagan suckled in a creed outworn;
> So might I, standing on this pleasant lea,
> Have glimpses that would make me less forlorn;
> Have sight of Proteus rising from the sea;
> Or hear old Triton blow his wreathed horn.[7]

More contemporary cultural narratives can figure in the thought component of nature appreciation too. For instance, it is common to see certain natural things as symbols of cherished cultural values. Mark Sagoff has documented how the raw landscape of America, lacking the rich historical narrative of Europe, was seen by its new inhabitants as a manifestation of the civic virtues of their new Republic, such as courage, innocence, freedom, strength, and the like. 'The paradigm, the symbol, if you will, of freedom', Sagoff writes, 'has been the wilderness, the deer, the bear, the eagle, a rapid river'.[8] When Americans found the opportunity to enjoy the wilderness, their experience was infused with thoughts of the civic virtues and the promise of the new nation.

Finally, moving still farther away from the realm of 'hard fact', we can identify fictional narratives as potential sources for the thought component of appreciation. Poets and novelists often depict fictional characters and events at real natural locations. When we turn to appreciate those actual landscapes, we may bring with us associations and ideas from those fictional works. Allen Carlson has described how Tony Hillerman's popular detective novels, set in the American south-west, have shaped their readers' aesthetic appreciation of that landscape.[9] Even without a fictional narrative for a guide, each of us may concoct a personal imaginative narrative to employ in appreciating a landscape. Emily Brady offers the example of imagining a locust tree, with its thick ridged bark, as a 'seasoned old man'.[10] Alternatively, we might see a natural rock formation as a human face, or a cloud formation as a distant mountain range.[11] Or, if we are in a playful mood, our narrative might be more ironic, seeing the cloud as a basket of washing, rather than a mountain range.[12] And in darker moods, our imagination may move in different directions, hearing the wind as a lonely sigh or an expression of nature's anger.

In short, the recognition that our experience of aesthetic qualities can contain, and be shaped by, a thought component reveals the potentially enormous range and variety possible in the aesthetic appreciation of nature.

A POST-MODERN APPROACH TO THE AESTHETICS OF NATURE

Our recognition of the potential variety of aesthetic responses to nature raises an important philosophical issue. What if, in responding aesthetically to a natural thing, different people bring different thoughts to bear on it, producing incompatible aesthetic evaluations of the same natural thing or phenomenon?

For example, imagine that Penny, Sam and Fred look up at the night sky. Penny sees the sky as filled with vivid pictures, much like a vast painting. In particular, she lets her mind wander through the tales of Greek mythology, imagining the stars as faithless lovers flung into the sky by the fickle gods. Tracing out the shape of the Great Bear, she pictures Jupiter rescuing Callisto from her son's arrows and then flinging her into the sky, where jealous Hera now eternally keeps her from rest.[13] Sam doesn't think of any of this, but rather muses on matters astronomical: the various cosmic structures visible in the pattern of the stars, such as the Milky Way, as well as the intricate movements of the planets, including our own, due to the action of gravitational forces. Fred, for his part, doesn't think about either mythology or astronomy. For Fred, the night sky consists merely of a pattern of lights. He doesn't even bother to think that the lights he sees *are stars*: to him, they are simply a wonderful pattern.

Penny, Sam and Fred each experience the night sky as having a certain aesthetic quality, or qualities, and each enjoys it for the particular quality or qualities that he or she sees in it. Penny, for instance, finds the night sky full of sadness and poignancy, a lonely gallery of mortals cruelly frozen, forever, in the heavens. Sam, on the other hand, sees the stars as elements in larger cosmic structures, and delights in the sublime vastness and manifold intricacy of these structures. Fred, in contrast to both, finds the night sky to look delicate and diaphanous, like a jewelled veil draped over the earth. In each case, the aesthetic qualities perceived differ, and this can be traced to different ways of thinking about the night sky. The sadness and poignancy that Penny perceives arises from what she imagines the patterns of the stars to be: namely, the outlines of the tragic figures of myth. Sam's perception of sublime intricacies in the night sky's patterns, on the other hand, emerges out of his thinking of the stars as elements in vast and complex cosmic structures. And Fred's appreciation of the night sky as delicate and diaphanous is tied to regarding the stars merely as elements in a two-dimensional pattern, rather than enormous galaxies or the frozen bodies of Greek lovers.

This sort of variation in aesthetic responses to the same natural thing raises a question that lies at the heart of our philosophical investigation, and with which we will be preoccupied for the next several chapters: namely, how we *ought* to appreciate nature aesthetically. A slightly different way of phrasing the question is as one about the place of concepts such as correctness and appropriateness in the aesthetic appreciation of nature.[14] Regarding the aesthetic judgements about the sky made by each of our appreciators, should we say that one of them is more correct than the others? Can we say that Penny, for example, has conceptualized the night sky more appropriately than Fred has, so that her aesthetic response to it is more appropriate than his? Or, alternatively, ought we to say that all of these different thought components, and the aesthetic judgements to which they lead, are equally valid?

Historically speaking, many philosophers have settled on an affirmative answer to this last question. On their view, when it comes to different thoughts that we may bring to an aesthetic appraisal of nature, anything goes. The Italian philosopher Benedetto Croce summed up this view nicely by saying that 'as regards natural beauty, man is like the mythical Narcissus at the fountain'.[15] This image is apt, according to Croce, because nature becomes beautiful (or, as we would prefer to say, aesthetically appealing) only when we 'dress it' with thoughts and associations that bestow meaning upon it. But we are free to bring whatever thoughts and associations we like to nature, and so, like Narcissus, what we see in nature is ultimately a reflection of ourselves – that is, our own inclinations and dispositions. As Croce puts it, 'the same natural object or fact is, according to the disposition of the soul, now expressive, now insignificant, now expressive of one definite thing, now of another, sad or glad, sublime or ridiculous, sweet or laughable'.[16] Croce's remark suggests that when people disagree over the aesthetic character of some natural thing, it is often because they differ in the imaginative associations that they bring, or fail to bring, to it. But these are irresolvable debates, since neither's imaginative associations are 'more correct' than the other's. 'They may dispute for ever', Croce tells us, 'but they will never agree, save when they are supplied with a sufficient dose of aesthetic knowledge to enable them to recognize that both are right'.[17]

This view of nature appreciation can be further illustrated by way of an analogy with a familiar view of the nature of art, a view that we can call 'Post-modernism'. 'Post-modernism' is a term that is used in different ways in different academic fields, but for our purposes we can focus on one important meaning of that term in literary theory. On this meaning, Post-modernism is the view that a literary work does not possess an inherent meaning (one assigned to it by the author, for instance) that a reader attempts to grasp.[18] Rather, the meaning of the work is created in the act of reading it, as the reader brings to the words on the page various associations and interpretations. This attitude towards literary works brings with it a certain freedom in interpreting and, hence, appreciating them: if there is no inherent meaning in the work itself, one is free to bring any associations or interpretations one wishes to it. Since the reader creates the text in the act of reading, it is, in the end, her text. As such, she is free to employ whatever materials she wishes.

Having introduced the post-modern view concerning art, we can now use it as an illuminating analogy for the 'anything goes' approach to appreciating nature. Just as we, as readers, actually create the literary text when we read it, so when we appreciate nature we actually compose the landscape.[19] This doesn't mean, of course, that when Penny looks up at the night sky, her gaze causes stars to come into being, any more than Post-modernism, in a literary context, entails that when you read a text you actually cause the words on the page to spring into existence. In each case, the physical things, the fiery gaseous bodies or the ink marks on the page, exist independently of our thinking about them; what we bring into being is the meaning or significance of the ink marks on the page and the fiery gaseous bodies. Because we create it, we are free to employ whatever thoughts we please in doing so. Based on this analogy, we will henceforth call the 'anything goes' view of nature appreciation the 'post-modern view'.

The post-modern approach to nature appreciation is appealing for a number of reasons. If the approach is right, then the aesthetic appreciation of nature turns out to be quite a free and stimulating sort of activity.[20] Rather than there being only one, or a small number, of correct ways to think about nature when aesthetically appreciating it, there is an unlimited number of such ways. If we really are free to bring any thought component at all to our appreciation of nature, there is little chance that we will become bored with appreciating nature. Relatively speaking, the night sky changes little from night to night, or even century to century for that matter, but we can always bring to it some new association or imaginative thought that may yield fresh delights. Thus the post-modern approach seems to explain, and legitimate, the perennial fascination that many of us find in watching clouds or the night sky.

This 'open-ended' character of nature appreciation may also make it more personally rewarding for us, in the sense of allowing us a chance to express and develop 'who we are'.[21] On the post-modern approach, when we engage in aesthetically appreciating a natural thing, we not only give meaning to the thing that we appreciate; we may also, in selecting that meaning, express and develop our own attitudes, values and beliefs. In drawing the analogy with Narcissus, Croce characterizes the appreciation of nature as looking in a mirror. But this does not quite do it justice, on the post-modern view. Our interest in natural things need not be just a passive reflection of our inclinations and dispositions, or what we might call our 'inward life', since we can actively choose which thoughts to apply to nature. Sometimes, what we find in nature engages and stimulates our imagination, challenging us to think differently and apply thoughts and associations in new situations and in new ways. In doing this, we can explore new dimensions of own inclinations and dispositions. The poetry of the Romantic Movement provides many examples of this imaginative struggle with nature: consider Shelley's encounter with Mont Blanc, or Wordsworth's moving reappraisal of his youthful haunt on the Wye river.[22] These cases are rare triumphs of the imagination, to be sure, but everyone is capable of thinking about nature with some measure of genuine creativity. When this happens, as Ronald Hepburn puts it, our appreciation of nature not only *displays* our inward life, it becomes a factor in *shaping* that inward life.[23]

OBJECTIONS TO THE POST-MODERN APPROACH

In spite of its virtues, however, philosophers have raised a number of important objections to the post-modern view. To begin putting the view into a critical perspective, consider again Post-modernism as a view about the aesthetic appreciation of art. According to that view, when it comes to thinking about the meaning of a literary text, we have a case of 'anything goes'. The reader is free to assign any particular meaning she likes, if she finds that reading the text with that meaning increases its aesthetic merit for her. But this view does not seem true to the facts about the actual evaluation of literary works. If we look at how people actually evaluate literary works, we see that it is not, in fact, a case of 'anything goes'. Imagine, for example, that Sally has just read Cervantes' *Don Quixote*.[24] When we ask for her appraisal of the novel, she says that she loved its ironical use of seventeenth-century language and its oblique references to the Russian Revolution. When we point out that Cervantes, the author of *Don Quixote*, actually lived in the seventeenth century, and so wasn't being ironic in using the language he did, and that the Russian Revolution occurred 200 years after *Don Quixote* was written, Sally says 'I know that; but I'm pretending that it was written by a jaded French novelist in 1935'. What are we to make of Sally's attitude here?

On one hand, Sally is of course free to take *Don Quixote* however she wants. But, on the other hand, many people would certainly have the intuition that there is something wrong with the way in which she has approached the book. Literary interpretation allows for a great deal of leeway, but we do not generally take seriously interpretations that distort the nature of the work *to this extent*. For example, when a literary critic wants to defend the merits of a book that someone thinks is vapid or poorly done, she may offer a new interpretation of it, trying to get the reader to see new significances or unnoticed depths in the events or characters. What she won't do is ask us to make believe it was written in a different century, or by a completely different person. Such interpretations lie outside the boundaries of what is considered an acceptable or serious interpretation. This is reflected in the fact that such interpretations don't find their way into the essays and books that constitute serious literary criticism. A different way to put the point is that Sally's interpretation, even if it allows us to get more enjoyment out of engaging with *Don Quixote* than we normally would get, is too far removed from the actual work to tell us anything about its merits. What we want to know, in appreciating *Don Quixote*, is how good the novel is, and Sally's view seems not to bear on this issue. It seems to tell us more about clever ways in which the work can be used than about the merit of the work itself.

What this suggests is that, as a characterization of the appreciation of art, Post-modernism is a mistaken view, at least in the extreme form that we have glossed it here. In appreciating art, we don't have a case of anything goes: the aesthetic appreciation of art is governed by some normative standards. These standards designate some ways of thinking about an artwork as simply incorrect or inappropriate, for the purposes of aesthetically appreciating the work.[25] Rejecting post-modernism in this way does not commit us to the existence of a single true meaning for any particular text, but it does entail that there are limits on acceptable interpretations. This reassessment of post-modernism about art prompts us to ask whether a post-modern approach can really do justice, after all, to the aesthetic appreciation of nature.[26]

The defender of the Post-modern approach to nature appreciation can appeal, however, to an important difference between art and nature. For our objection to the Post-modernist view about art was based on a comparison of that view with general facts regarding the practice of literary criticism. In particular, it was based on the fact that, actually, not anything goes in the practice of literary criticism. Rather, there do seem to be some normative standards that rule out at least *some* interpretations as inappropriate. But in the case of nature, one might argue, the situation is quite different. In the case of our aesthetic experience of nature, for example, it is not clear that there is even anything parallel to the practice of art criticism. In the world of art, criticism occurs at both an informal level, where individuals come together to discuss and argue the merits of books and films at cocktail parties and book clubs, and a professional level, where critics with some relevant training and experience write formal appraisals for publication. But what is there that is analogous to all this in the realm of nature appreciation? There are not obvious instances of debate and appraisal, where different judgements about the aesthetic character of nature are evaluated. People delight in mountain peaks or revile the look of swamps, but they do so on their own, or in extremely informal contexts: there are no clubs or journals where the aesthetic merits of different mountain peaks are debated or systematically explored, for instance. These differences are also readily explicable, for we can easily understand why critical disputes arise more frequently and naturally with art than with nature. For example, artists often dispute criticism of their work. Nature, of course, cannot 'speak up' in this way, and so disputes about the aesthetic merits of natural things and places are apt to be less frequent. But, in any event, to the extent that it is true that there is nothing analogous to the practice of art criticism in the realm of nature appreciation, it may seem that nature appreciation must be a case of 'anything goes', even if art appreciation is not.

Even if the premise of this argument is true, however, it faces a serious objection, which we can introduce using an analogy from moral philosophy: the ethics of our treatment of non-human animals. Human relations are certainly governed by normative standards: rules that designate certain actions, such as theft and assault, as inappropriate or unacceptable. But are our relations with non-human animals governed by analogous normative standards? Or are they a matter of 'anything goes'? Traditionally, many people have held the latter view. Further, one can easily understand why people might have thought this. Since non-human animals, unlike humans, cannot 'speak out', disputes about their treatment have arisen less frequently. But that does not show that normative standards *ought* not to apply to human–animal relations. In this case, the question of the existence of normative standards ought to be addressed, as it usually now is, by considering the analogy between the treatment of animals and other behaviour that *is* subject to normative constraint (e.g. the treatment of humans). If non-human animals are similar enough to humans, then we ought to extend our normative standards to their treatment as well. If we do not, we stand accused of being arbitrary in treating one case differently for no good reason.[27]

If we apply this reasoning to the case of nature appreciation, we get what we can call the 'analogy with art argument' against Post-modernism.[28] The post-modern view assumes that we are to have normative standards for one, but not the other, of art and nature. But then, why art, after all? In the case of *Don Quixote*, it seemed bizarre to think that someone might seriously try to appreciate this artwork by concocting a fictitious story about its origins. Yet, in appreciating the night sky, this is more or less what Penny does when she conceptualizes the stars in terms of the stories of Greek myth. So why is this kind of appreciation not appropriate in the case of art, but fine in the case of nature? We can surely cite some factors, such as natural things not having an 'author', that explain the lack of critical debate and normative standards for nature. But however well factors of this sort *explain* the lack of normative standards for the aesthetics of nature, they seem insufficient to *justify* it. The analogy with art argument holds, then, that it is arbitrary to take the 'anything goes' view with respect to nature, but not with respect to art, unless some relevant difference between the two is specified. The argument pushes us, then, to look at the appreciation of nature in a different way than the post-modern view recommends. Instead of an exercise in imagination, or an exploration of our own beliefs and attitudes, we ought to approach it as an attempt to evaluate an object, albeit a natural one rather than artwork. Even if a body of 'nature criticism' does not currently exist, this does not mean there ought not to be one. Such a critical practice might, in fact, help us better articulate our aesthetic experiences of nature.[29]

Another set of arguments against the post-modern view pushes us toward the same conclusion, but based on more straightforwardly ethical considerations, rather than a comparison to art. The basic idea behind these arguments is that looking at the aesthetic appreciation of nature as a case of 'anything goes' is ethically problematic. This claim can be developed in a number of ways. One might argue that treating nature as a 'blank slate' on which we can project concepts and associations as we like manifests a casual disregard, or lack of respect, for nature.[30] Here again Croce's metaphor of nature appreciation as 'like the mythical Narcissus at the fountain' is instructive, for we typically view narcissism as a vice, a shallow absorption in one's own interests in contexts where it is appropriate to recognize others' interests. What the narcissist lacks is described by Yuriko Saito as 'a moral capacity of recognizing and understanding the other's reality through sympathetic imagination'.[31] It is not hard to find cases of nature appreciation that seem cast in this mould: seeing a pair of peaks in the Teton Range as a gigantic set of breasts, treating an old-growth forest as haunted, or imagining a falling star to be a message from one's lover, for examples. In these kinds of appreciation, the appreciator focuses on her own imagination without really recognizing the natural things involved. The first way of developing an ethical argument against the post-modernist approach, then, is to argue that adopting an attitude of respect for natural things by appreciating them 'on their own terms', as Saito puts it, is a moral virtue. Post-modernist appreciation fails to manifest this attitude, since it licences us to treat natural things merely as props for our self-indulgent fantasies: hence, it is flawed on ethical grounds.

In describing this attitude as one of 'respect for nature', however, it is important to contrast it with some other senses of that phrase. In environmental philosophy, for example, the idea of respect for nature figures as the central notion in Paul Taylor's well-known 'biocentric ethic'.[32] The concept of respect for nature, as Taylor employs it, has strong presuppositions and strong implications. Regarding the former, respect for nature, in Taylor's sense, is based on the presumption of the equal inherent worth of all species: we respect other species because each is as inherently worthy, in its own way, as our own. Regarding its implications, respect for nature, in Taylor's sense, places strong ethical obligations on us, in our treatment of other species: we have duties to refrain from interfering with other species and to compensate them for any harm that we inflict upon them, for example.[33]

The attitude of respect that is at issue in the ethical argument discussed above, in contrast, lacks these strong presumptions and strong implications. One can regard natural things 'on their own terms' without believing that each of them has an equal inherent worth. Also, regarding things on their own terms does not, in itself, entail that one adopts any particular course of action with respect to them. Our treatment of persons is a good example here: say that you agree to take person X on his own terms, just as he is, as an honest and trusting, but not too bright, fellow. If you happen to be a thief, you might decide to try con person X, precisely because of the sort of person he is. The point of this example is not to show that it is ethically acceptable to steal, but to show that just taking things on their own terms is not enough to determine a ethical course of action with regard to them. The thief takes people as they are, and so he doesn't possess the particular ethical flaw of failing to take others on their own terms, but he is still morally flawed, since he fails to recognize other sound ethical principles (e.g. do not take advantage of others for your own gain) that should guide his actions. The same point applies to nature. Rejecting sentimental characterizations of non-human animals and insisting on regarding them in light of what we know about their actual habits, behaviour and nature, while a virtue, is compatible with all sorts of different ways of treating them.[34] To put it differently, although the absence of narcissism makes one ethically better than one would be otherwise, it does not entail much about what one's overall conduct will be like, nor is it sufficient to ensure that that conduct will be particularly ethically worthy.

Nonetheless, the idea that manifesting this particular kind of respect for nature is a ethical virtue still throws a different light on a supposed advantage of the post-modern view: its capacity to maximize our aesthetic enjoyment and afford us the opportunity to develop richer inner lives. On this line of thought, focusing only on these advantages neglects the fact that aesthetic appreciation of nature involves more than us – it involves nature as well. The post-modern attitude may be better for us, in some sense, but ethical considerations mean that we must consider more than just ourselves.

The ethical argument against the post-modern view can also be developed in a second, slightly different way. In addition to arguing that appreciating nature in the 'anything goes' fashion is an unethical way to behave, one can argue that it is ethically problematic insofar as it ultimately results in harmful consequences for the environment. This can

happen directly, as when too much of a focus on imaginative appreciation causes us to lose touch with, and mistreat, nature.[35] As an example
of this, Marcia Eaton cites the influence of the 1942 film *Bambi* on attitudes towards deer management in the United States.[36] The unforgettable
depiction of gentle, harmless creatures existing in harmony with nature
deeply influenced the way most of us see deer. As Eaton puts it, when we
see deer, what we see are cuddly and kind guardians of nature. Unfortu-
nately, however, reality is more complex. When unchecked, deer can
overrun local ecosystems, resulting in disaster for other species, such as
some songbirds. But the conception of deer imbued by *Bambi*, albeit
a fictitious one, has made it hard to convince the public that, in certain
contexts, deer populations need to be culled. In cases like this, the
environment itself can be the direct victim of overly sentimental appreciation.

Finally, there is a third way in which the ethical argument against the
post-modern approach to nature appreciation can be developed. This is
as the charge that an 'anything goes' approach to appreciating nature
stultifies the use of aesthetic value in environmental decision making. In
particular, it stymies what is sometimes called 'Aesthetic Preservation':
the appeal to the aesthetic merit of natural areas as a reason for preserving them from exploitation or development. Think back to Sagoff's idea,
discussed earlier in this chapter, that we should see natural things as
symbols of certain basic values, seeing, for example, the eagle as a
symbol of freedom. One might appeal to this idea to argue for the preservation or protection of natural things, including particular landscapes
or species. Sagoff writes that 'a society which values freedom and which
makes its forests or the wildlife in them the expressive symbols of freedom will not treat the wildlife in them frivolously, nor discard them
without a second thought.'[37] On the post-modern view, however, any
such argument becomes highly problematic. For on that view, any way of
thinking of a natural thing is as good, for the purposes of aesthetic appreciation, as any other. If a developer looks at the eagle and sees, not a
symbol of freedom, but a symbol of predatory elitism, then she may
disagree with the claim that it is aesthetically good, and so worth preserving. On the post-modern view, this sort of debate over aesthetic
character cannot be resolved. The upshot is that, for the purposes of arguing for the preservation of nature, claims about nature's aesthetic
character become useless. The strength of this objection ultimately
depends upon whether Aesthetic Preservation is itself a viable idea. This
is a large issue, which we will examine in detail in Chapter 7. For the

moment, we need only note that, whatever other difficulties this approach to preservation might face, the post-modern approach adds to them.

If these objections are compelling, we will want to reject the post-modernist's claim, that all thought components in aesthetic appreciation are equally appropriate, as too extreme. We will want to insist that, as in the case of art, the thought component we bring to appreciation cannot be just anything at all – some forms of thinking lead us astray, distorting the thing that we are trying to appreciate. But what sort of thinking, then, is the appropriate kind? How ought we to aesthetically appreciate nature? In the following three chapters, we will examine three very different answers to this question, beginning, in the next chapter, with the view known as Formalism.

CHAPTER 3

FORMALISM

In the previous chapter, we examined one approach to the aesthetics of nature: the post-modern approach. If we reject this approach, then we assert that not all ways of thinking about a natural thing are equally valid for the purpose of aesthetically appreciating it. In order for aesthetic appreciation to be *appropriate*, we need to conceptualize nature in the correct way. But then what *is* the correct way? One important answer to this question is provided by the view known as Formalism: the correct way to think about nature is as a perceptual array of pure lines, shapes and colours – in other words, as 'pure form'.[1] In this chapter, we will explore this view, assessing its strengths and weaknesses.

FORMALISM, NATURE AND PICTURES

We can illustrate the formalist approach by returning to our example of the appreciation of the night sky, which we used to characterize the post-modern view in the previous chapter. Penny, Sam and Fred all enjoy the stars aesthetically, but each brings a different thought component to his or her appreciation. Penny ruminates on the tales of mythology, Sam sees the stars as elements in larger astronomical structures and Fred enjoys the night sky simply for the pleasing pattern formed by the innumerable spots of light. The formalist's view is that Fred's appreciation is the more appropriate or correct one, for Fred delights in the stars simply as pleasing visual patterns – arrays of line, shape and colour – and nothing more. By thinking of the stars as mythological characters, or as elements of some vast cosmic structure, Penny and Sam each engage in a less appropriate form of appreciation. To put it differently, each of them captures less of the genuine aesthetic character of the night sky than Fred does.

At first glance, this may appear somewhat counter-intuitive. After all, Fred really isn't thinking much at all when he appreciates the stars. He is 'just looking'. Penny and Sam, on the other hand, each brings a rich thought component to their appreciation. Yet his or her appreciation is said to be deficient in comparison to Fred's. It may seem puzzling that a richer and more sophisticated thought component could result in *less* appropriate appreciation. After all, Penny and Sam can plausibly be said to see a great deal more in the sky than Fred does. But according to the formalist, this puzzlement arises from thinking along the lines of the post-modern model, where the central aim of aesthetic appreciation is to maximize our aesthetic enjoyment, or perhaps to explore our inner lives, by imposing whatever conceptions we wish onto nature. According to the formalist, this is not the central aim of aesthetic appreciation. Rather, the central aim is for us to evaluate the aesthetic qualities of natural things. And doing this, she claims, requires bringing a smaller, more austere thought component to our appreciation, rather than a richer one. What this requires is precisely the attentive act of 'just looking' that Fred performs.

But why does the formalist think that the correct way to think of nature, for the purposes of aesthetic appreciation, is simply as a pure array of line, shape and colour? This view can be justified by invoking some version of the idea, introduced in Chapter 1, that aesthetic appreciation is 'disinterested', requiring a detachment from our own desires. In aesthetically appreciating a landscape, for example, the imperative of disinterestedness requires us to enjoy it for its own sake, rather than for the benefits that it has for us. This idea leads towards Formalism because one way to ensure that we enjoy the perceptual appearance of the object for its own sake, and not for the sake of any practical benefit it brings us, is for us to just empty our heads of thoughts about the object and what it might be good for. If we put aside thoughts about what the object is, and what it does, and focus only on its perceptual appearance, or its 'form', then there will be no danger of our taking surreptitious pleasure in the benefits that the object promises. Our delight then can spring only from the perceptual appearance of the object, because that appearance will be the only thing we are thinking about. To borrow a nice phrase from the eighteenth-century philosopher Archibald Alison, we can say that the mind is best equipped to aesthetically appreciate nature when it is 'vacant and unemployed', uncluttered by thoughts about it. In this way, Formalism can be seen as diametrically opposed to the post-modern approach. Rather than embracing the wide variety of thoughts that we might employ in aesthetic appreciation, Formalism holds that we ought to eschew it, focusing only on the perceptual appearance itself – that is, on the lines, shapes and colours that we perceive immediately.

Formalism has been very influential in thinking about the aesthetic appreciation of art. In the early twentieth century, the British art critic Clive Bell developed Formalism as a way of approaching the work of post-impressionist painters, such as Paul Cézanne. Bell thought that, unlike many traditional artists, the post-impressionists were not aiming primarily at representing characters and events, depicting a story, or even representing ideas, but at producing 'lines and colours combined in a particular way, certain forms and relations of forms'.[2] In the art of these painters, the actual objects represented were unimportant: what counted were the pure forms they produced in painting them. Bell viewed the achievement of the post-impressionists not only as a shift in artistic practice, however, but also as a fundamental discovery of the true nature of art and aesthetic experience. By allowing the shapes and patterns in a painting to call to our mind thoughts of characters and events, emotions and ideas, we prevent ourselves from appreciating art aesthetically. Bell acknowledges that we often do think about what artworks represent, but argues that such thoughts are always 'irrelevant' to aesthetic appreciation. Appropriate appreciation must focus on the pure form alone, and to appreciate this, Bell tells us, 'we need bring with us nothing but a sense of form and colour and a knowledge of three-dimensional space'.[3]

Although Bell was primarily interested in the appreciation of visual art, he does mention the possibility of appreciating nature aesthetically. He writes:

> Who has not, once at least in his life, had a sudden vision of landscape as pure form? For once, instead of seeing it as fields and cottages, he has felt it as lines and colours . . . Is it not clear that he has won from material beauty the thrill that, generally, art alone can give, because he has contrived to see it as a pure formal combination of lines and colours?[4]

On Bell's view, the aesthetic appreciation of nature involves the same fundamental activity as that of art: seeing an object as pure form. But aesthetically appreciating nature, he insists, is much more difficult and rare than the aesthetic appreciation of art.[5] Bell's point makes perfect sense, given the differences between paintings and landscapes. It is not that difficult to stand in an art gallery and see a painting by Cézanne as a pure assemblage of lines, shapes and colours, rather than as a house beside a mountain, although Bell thinks that this too takes a good deal of effort. But it is much more difficult to get oneself to see an *actual* mountain as nothing more than a 'pure formal combination of lines and colours'. For an actual landscape is not a painting: it is not small, neatly packaged in a frame and easily taken in at a glance. On the contrary, it is vast and enveloping. It can be hard to see where the various shapes begin and end, and hard to determine what is part of the object and what is not. Furthermore, unlike a painting, a natural thing such as a mountain changes its look over time, and even from moment to moment as light and atmospheric conditions change. Often, we ourselves alter its appearance by moving in relation to it: we may get closer to it, or change the angle from which we view it, for instance.[6] And finally, landscapes cannot be sequestered in the calm and controlled environment of the art gallery. Nature continually reminds us that its landscapes are *not* a mere assemblage of lines, shapes and colours by blowing wind in our faces, pelting us with rain and jostling us in various other ways.

While accepting these facts about the aesthetic appreciation of nature, the formalist will point out, however, that the difficulties they create are by no means insurmountable. In fact, she can point out that we have developed ways of facilitating what Bell called the 'vision of landscape as pure form'. Take the scenic look-off, as an example. The scenic look-off is a certain spot, such as a roadside turnout on a highway, chosen certainally to allow a viewer to compose the elements of the surrounding landscape into a fine 'picture'. The position of a look-off in a mountain pass, for example, can be selected to allow the shapes of the various mountains to balance one another, or to allow the observer to see a pleasing diversity of shapes (letting him catch a glimpse of the shimmering river in the corner of scene), and so forth. Also, the scenic look-off is meant to reproduce for the viewer something of the calm of the art gallery. Nature may still pelt us with distracting wind and rain, but parked on the look-off we can at least avoid being distracted by our own motion, or by the need to fight through the terrain in order to see the natural scene. We can focus our attention, for a few quiet moments, on the assemblage of lines, shapes and colours laid out before us. In a sense, the scenic look-off does turn nature into something like an enormous, three-dimensional painting, laid out for our enjoyment. There is even an 'artist' of a sort – the creator or designer of the look-off – who, even if he doesn't create the elements of the view, deliberately chooses the way they will be arranged into the final product that is taken in by the viewer.

The formalist approach to aesthetic appreciation that seems to underlie the modern practice of the scenic look-off can be traced back to the emergence of a taste for picturesque landscape in the eighteenth century, a phenomenon that was discussed in Chapter 1.[7] The picturesque involved a delight in qualities such as irregularity, roughness of texture and sudden variation, and was introduced to the popular taste through the dissemination of landscape paintings that emphasized these qualities. But the taste for the picturesque was not only inspired by the *content* of these pictures (i.e. the actual landscapes depicted); often, the idea was that a picturesque landscape was one that literally resembled such a picture.[8] Accordingly, we find in the eighteenth-century picturesque an early movement towards something like the scenic look-off: a place that presents nature's lines, shapes and colours in optimal configuration and with a minimum of distraction. An example of this is Rievaulx Terrace, the large, landscaped terrace built by the Englishman Thomas Duncombe III overlooking his estate in Yorkshire. Describing the terrace, Stephanie Ross writes that 'in creating his terrace [Duncombe] appropriated that view and framed it in a way that controlled and orchestrated each viewer's experience'.[9]

In addition, the picturesque approach had even more convenient means for facilitating the 'vision of landscape as pure form': devices such as the Claude mirror and the Claude glass.[10] The Claude mirror is a small tinted convex mirror used to reflect a landscape. The observer stands, her back to the landscape, and observes it in the mirror, which alters its appearance to more closely resemble a landscape painting. Although artists found the Claude mirror useful in painting landscapes, enthusiasts of the picturesque, such as Thomas West and William Gilpin, recommended that tourists and sightseers also use it as a tool for 'improving' the look of actual landscapes.[11] As West describes, in his popular guidebook for the English Lake District, 'where the objects are great and near, [the mirror] removes them to a due distance, and shows them in the soft colours of nature, and in the most regular perspective the eye can perceive, or science demonstrate'.[12]

Today, the Claude mirror is no more than a historical curiosity, and the feverish enthusiasm for picturesque scenery and landscape painting that fuelled its popularity has long since petered out. But the formalist will insist that the underlying idea of the picturesque – the notion that nature should be appreciated, more or less, like a set of large, out-of-doors pictures – is very much alive. In our culture the picturesque has evolved into what Donald Crawford calls the 'postcardesque'.[13] The landscape painting has been replaced by the picture postcard, which serves a similar function as the tourist's ideal of aesthetic excellence in nature. The postcard captures, in a portable and easily reproduced fashion, the carefully orchestrated arrangement of lines, shapes and colours that the scenic look-off allows us to experience in person. On the formalist view, the existence of the postcardesque mode of nature appreciation is very much to the good. By encouraging us to treat nature more like a picture, it helps us to focus solely on its pure form, and hence truly appreciate its aesthetic character, extending the sort of delight that we normally take only in art to the natural as well.

STRENGTHS OF FORMALISM

The formalist's approach to the aesthetics of nature possesses a number of strengths. First, it can claim to illuminate and explain much of what people actually do in aesthetically appreciating nature. As mentioned above, the more or less standard tourist routine of stopping at a scenic look-off, 'taking it all in', snapping a photo and then buying the professionally rendered picture postcard image at a nearby gift shop makes perfect sense from the formalist perspective. Furthermore, Formalism allows us to make sense of the fact that most tourists aesthetically appreciate nature without bringing much of a thought component to what they appreciate. The motorist who pulls over at the roadside turnout for a brief look at a mountain valley below may not think of much at all, but simply 'take a look', much as Fred, in our previous example, simply looked at the pattern of the starry skies. It is true that roadside turnouts sometimes present plaques that convey historical or scientific information about the view before us, but the formalist will see these as inessential for appreciating the *aesthetic* character of the scene. We may take in the offered information, if we happen to be interested in science or history, but we can also choose to simply enjoy the scene aesthetically, without thinking about where the forests and mountains before us came from, what they are like or even what they are, aside from pure combinations of lines, shapes and colours.

Formalism also cleaves to another idea that many people have about the aesthetic character of nature: namely, that it provides an escape from daily life, and the spheres of society, family and work that we all inhabit for most of the time. In the popular imagination and in glossy tourist ads, 'natural beauty' is often associated with rejuvenation, relaxation and spiritual renewal. For many of us, gazing at the stars, spending a few minutes just staring up at the clouds or watching the waves roll in on a quiet beach are ways to leave behind our worries and 'recharge our batteries', as the expression goes. On the formalist view, we can see why this would be. When we aesthetically appreciate things, we attend solely to their perceptual form, leaving behind other thoughts and distractions.

Bell, in his description of the aesthetic appreciation of art, elegantly captures this idea of aesthetic appreciation as a retreat or escape. He writes that: 'Art transports us from the world of man's activity to a world of aesthetic exaltation. For a moment we are shut off from human interests; our anticipations and memories are arrested; we are lifted above the stream of life'.[14]

Bell speaks here of art, but the aesthetic appreciation of nature would seem to have the same power to transport us to 'a world of aesthetic exaltation'. Indeed, one might even think that the aesthetic appreciation of nature has greater potential for doing so, since in appreciating art, even if we succeed in reducing a painting to pure line, shape and colour, we remain in the presence of something artefactual, an element of the human world. When we appreciate nature aesthetically, we move beyond this world. The idea of aesthetic appreciation as an escape or retreat thus helps to explain why we value the aesthetic appreciation of nature to the extent that we do. It allows us an experience of purity and simplicity in which we can rediscover, as Nick Zangwill puts it, our sense of 'childlike wonder' at the world around us.[15]

Formalism also allows us to make sense of the important interrelations that exist between art and the aesthetic appreciation of nature. As we have seen, landscape painting played a vital role in the development of tastes for landscape in modern Europe. Eighteenth-century observers learned to take aesthetic pleasure in new forms of landscape once painters had shown the way by depicting those forms. This phenomenon persists today. As Robert Stecker puts it, often we find that 'a painting (or more usually) a style of painting provides a new way of seeing while also enabling one to see the sights around one in a new way'.[16] In our post-cardesque culture, we could extend the point also to photography, such as the work of Ansel Adams, but the general point is the same: art often expands and enriches our aesthetic appreciation of nature. On the formalist's view, this is just what one would expect, since the principal business of the artist, on that view, is to produce pleasing form. The artist learns, by theory and practice, which configurations of lines, which arrangements of shapes and which distributions of colours best please the eye. So it stands to reason that the artist, more than anyone else, would be the person best equipped to help us identify pleasing form in the natural realm. Indeed, it is no surprise that the formalist view finds many important connections between the aesthetics of art and the aesthetics of nature. For on the formalist view, to aesthetically appreciate nature is more or less to treat it as we treat works of art: as we would treat a large, out-of-doors painting or sculpture.

Perhaps even more important than these various factors, however, in the case for Formalism, is the ability of Formalism to answer two important objections to the post-modern approach to the aesthetics of nature. The first of these is what we called the analogy with art argument. The argument is that if not all aesthetic responses to an artwork are equally valid or appropriate then the same ought to hold for our aesthetic responses to nature, in the absence of any good reason for their differing in this basic way. Formalists can answer this argument by claiming that, for both art and nature, there are some aesthetic responses that are more appropriate or valid: namely, those that are based only on a scrutiny of the pure form of the object. The formalist's treatment of the aesthetic character of nature, then, cannot be said to be arbitrary or unprincipled, since she extends the same view to nature as she does to art. Again, this feature flows naturally out of the fact that to aesthetically appreciate nature, for the formalist, is more or less to treat nature as we would a work of art.

Formalists can also reply to the ethical objections against the post-modern model. Recall that one of those objections was that, by taking the aesthetic appreciation of nature to be an 'anything goes' affair, the post-modern view renders aesthetic value useless in debates about environmental preservation. If every way of thinking about a natural thing is equally valid, for the purposes of aesthetic appreciation, then individuals who think differently about a particular natural thing can have irresolvable differences over its aesthetic value. When Jane sees a horse as aesthetically excellent, and James sees it as aesthetically poor because they differ in the way they conceptualize the thing, there simply is no basis on which we could say one is correct. This being the case, appeals to the aesthetic value of natural things become useless in environmental debates. But the formalist approach has it otherwise. There is a more appropriate or correct way of appreciating the aesthetic value of the horse: namely, an appreciation of its pure form – its line, shape and colour. Some animals, it might be claimed, have pleasing forms, while others do not.[17] If the horse has a pure form that is pleasing, then it really is aesthetically good: Jane is right and James is wrong. There are, in other words, better and worse answers to questions about the aesthetic value of a particular natural thing. This being the case, aesthetic value should not be simply dismissed altogether as useless in environmental debates, at least not on the grounds that disputes concerning it are irresolvable in principle.

However, the fact that there are 'genuine answers' to questions about the aesthetic value of natural things, in itself, might not get us very far in making aesthetic value useful in environmental debates. For in such debates, aesthetic value will have to be weighed against such things as the economic benefits that flow from developing or destroying nature rather than preserving it. These factors have the very important advantage of being quantifiable: the economic benefit of developing a mountain into a ski resort, for example, can be reduced to a simple, easily understood dollar figure. This makes such factors extremely attractive for use in making environmental management decisions, since decision makers can point to 'hard figures' as the basis for environmental policies. In contrast, even if one can say that the mountain really does have aesthetic value – that is, it really does have a pleasing form – this factor is less likely to carry weight unless it can be quantified and set against competing factors. As one commentator on the use of aesthetic value in environmental policy writes: 'It is not sufficient to determine which landscape condition is aesthetically better, we must also know how much better'.[18]

But here again Formalism seems to offer a solution. For according to Formalism, the aesthetic value of a natural scene, like the aesthetic value of an artwork, such as a painting, comes down to the particular array of lines, shapes and colours that it presents to the viewer's eye. By insisting that appropriate aesthetic response is devoid of a substantial thought component, formalists reduce the aesthetic value of a scene to these visual elements. But these visual elements can be quantified. Professionals in land management have developed a number of different techniques for doing this, but one common way involves the use of photographs to measure the visual parameters of natural views. Photographs of the natural area are taken, and geometrical techniques applied to them to measure different formal elements: the curvature of lines, the diversity of shapes, the gradations of colour and texture, and so forth. Once quantified, these elements can then be used to calculate an overall numerical value for the aesthetic value of the landscape in question. Daniel provides a succinct description of the process:

> The biophysical features of the landscape (mountains, lakes, trees, etc.) are translated into formal features (e.g. *form*, *line*, *texture*, *color*) and relationships among these features (e.g. *variety*, *unity*,

vividnesst [*sic*], *harmony*). Then, following prescribed rules and guidelines, areas are ranked from low to high quality (*visual quality* or *scenic class*).[19]

Using photographs to quantify the pure form of a natural scene in this way is not a trivial task, and the procedure raises some difficult questions. For instance, in assessing the aesthetic value of a natural thing or area that can be seen from different angles, where ought one to take the photographs? What weight should be accorded to each of the different formal features in determining overall visual quality? But these issues, difficult as they may be to resolve, are mainly ones of detail in the sense that they can be tackled through further empirical research. If the formalist approach is correct, then the general idea of quantifying nature's aesthetic value is sound. Furthermore, the advantages of being able to quantify nature's aesthetic value provide a strong motivation for tackling the issues of detail through further empirical study. If they can be resolved, then the aesthetic value of nature need not be regarded as the nebulous, subjective affair that it seems to be on the post-modern view. It will, on the contrary, be a matter of measurable facts, and therefore something to which we can appeal, without shame, in debates over environmental preservation.

OBJECTIONS TO FORMALISM

The considerations discussed in the previous section make Formalism an attractive view, and one can see its influence in many contemporary discussions of the aesthetics of nature. But serious objections have been raised to Formalism as a theory of the aesthetic appreciation of nature. The first of these objections is the claim that, even when we are appreciating artworks, the attentive scrutiny of pure form – arrangements of line, colour and shape – does not constitute appropriate aesthetic appreciation. In other words, if we do no more than 'just look' we will *miss* the work's true aesthetic qualities.

Philosophers have argued for this claim in different ways. Taking up examples from contemporary art, Arthur Danto notes that the 'pure form' of artworks – the arrays of line, shape and colour that they offer to the eye – are often relatively unimportant. A larger part of the work is constituted by the *meaning* that those arrays take on in light of the artist's intentions, or some body of art theory that pertains to the work. Danto offers the example of an imaginary series of visually indiscernible paintings, each consisting of a uniform red square.[20] The first painting is *Kierkegaard's Mood*, a work based on the choleric philosopher's description of his troubled state of mind. The second is *The Israelites Crossing the Red Sea*, a work that the artist explains by saying 'The Israelites had already crossed over, and the Egyptians were drowned'. The final work, *Nirvana*, is 'a metaphysical painting based on the artist's knowledge that the Nirvanic and Samsara orders are identical, and that the Samsara world is fondly called the Red Dust by its deprecators'.[21] Danto points out that these are very different artworks: the first is a psychological portrait, the second a historical painting and the third a piece of religious art. In virtue of these differences, they have very different aesthetic qualities. *Nirvana* has a serene, contemplative quality, for example, whereas *Kierkegaard's Mood* is just the opposite. What this shows is that the aesthetic character of a work depends upon more than its pure form – it depends upon a rich thought component that the appreciator brings to the work and which generates the meaning of the work's form.

The formalist, of course, might reply that it would be silly to claim, as Danto does, that these are 'different' works, having different aesthetic qualities. They all have an identical perceptual form, and so, the formalist might insist, we ought to say that they have the same aesthetic qualities: none is any more or less serene than any other, for example. The trouble with this reply is that it clashes dramatically with the way in which we actually treat contemporary art. The appreciation of contemporary artworks regularly extends far beyond a consideration of their pure form. Many contemporary artworks appear, to a first glance, to have no aesthetic qualities at all. Yet credible art critics insist that, when appreciated in light of art theory, they do possess aesthetic qualities. A recent poll of art experts, for instance, determined that the most influential artwork of the twentieth century is Marcel Duchamp's 1917 work *Fountain*, which consisted of a urinal with the word 'R. Mutt' scrawled on it.[22] Although it is conceivable that the pure form of *Fountain* (the colour of its porcelain, for instance) has some aesthetic appeal, it seems that the visual impact of this work cannot be explained by its 'pure form' alone. In light of examples such as these, Formalism might be seen as simply failing to fit the facts regarding our practice of art appreciation.

In fact, we need not even turn to controversial cases of modern art to justify the conclusion that Formalism does not adequately describe the aesthetic qualities of artworks. Kendall Walton, for example, argues that some of an artwork's aesthetic qualities can only be perceived if our perception involves, as part of our thought component, information about the work's genre or artistic category. Consider, for example, aesthetically appreciating a marble bust.[23] Depending on the particular characteristics of the work, we might describe one particular marble bust as 'serene', and another as 'rugged' or 'harsh-looking'. But when we make these sorts of aesthetic assessments of marble busts, we typically do not do so, even in part, based on the fact that they are abruptly broken off at the chest. But why is that? The abrupt break at the chest is, after all, a part of the 'pure form' of the work: it constitutes one part of the array of lines and shapes that the work presents to the eye. But no one would argue that a particular bust is rugged, or harsh looking, because its lines abruptly break off at the chest. If someone *did* argue this, we would say he simply misunderstood what it was that he was looking at. A bust can be rugged looking in virtue of the expressive qualities of the face it represents, or, perhaps, the style employed in rendering it, but not in virtue of being broken off at the chest. For being broken off at the chest is just a universal feature of marble busts, part of what makes them busts. In other words, a consideration of the pure form of the work alone, without a thought component that extends beyond this form, misleads us as to the aesthetic qualities of the work of art. In order to appropriately appreciate the work, we have to bring, to our appreciation, knowledge of the sort of artwork that we are looking at, knowledge that guides us in choosing the aspects of sensory form to which we ought to attend, and how we ought to attend to them.

We can sum up this line of thought by saying that Formalism ultimately fails as a theory of appropriate aesthetic appreciation of art because, in its insistence that appreciation utilize only a very austere thought component, it distorts the nature of art. When we attend to pure form, what we get is not an appreciation of the artwork, but at most an appreciation of a set of perceptual impressions produced by the artwork. Since an artwork is more than a set of perceptual impressions, more than 'just looking' at the pure form is needed to appreciate it. A thought component that includes some richer conception of the nature of the work is also necessary.

If this line of thought about art is correct, then Formalism about the aesthetic appreciation of nature must be seriously called into question as well. For nature, too, is more than a set of perceptual impressions. A mountain valley, for example, is not simply an assemblage of lines, shapes and colours. And as such, one might argue that to appreciate it as merely a set of perceptual impressions is to distort its aesthetic qualities, just as treating an artwork as a set of perceptual impressions distorts its aesthetic qualities. If we look only at these perceptual impressions, what we end up appreciating is, in Hepburn's words, not nature itself, but 'nature dissolving, fragmenting to kaleidoscopic splinters'.[24] Consider again Hepburn's example of appreciating a falling autumn leaf. The formalist would have us dismiss thoughts of the leaf as a symbol of the transience of life, and attend solely to the leaf's shape and colour, reducing it to 'a small, fluttering, reddish-brown material object – and no more'.[25] But this conception of the leaf seems, as Hepburn says, 'unacceptably thin', because a leaf is more than a small, fluttering, reddish-brown material object. Further, when we aesthetically appreciate art, we balk at restricting ourselves to such a thin conception – why should we accept it for nature?

In fact, one might argue that the formalist approach distorts the character of nature to a much greater degree than it distorts the nature of art. This is because appreciating art in a formal fashion, while it involves ignoring important aspects of artworks, at least allows one to remain more or less in physical proximity to what one is appreciating. In the case of appreciating landscapes, however, engaging in the formal sort of aesthetic appreciation typically involves withdrawing to a distance where one can 'take it all in' visually, and where one is somewhat removed from elements that distract one's attention, such as wind, rain, the scratching of tree branches and one's own movement. But in doing this, we lose contact with the very thing we are trying to appreciate – that is, we withdraw from the landscape itself.[26] Consequently, in putting ourselves in a position to take in the pure form of the mountain valley, by driving to a scenic look-off some miles away, for instance, we end up completely missing most of the aesthetic qualities of that valley. We become unable to tell what trees it contains, what animals inhabit it, and so forth. We see only a small portion of its aesthetic offerings. Thus the formalist approach does not improve our aesthetic appreciation of the forest, but rather impoverishes it.

The basic flaw in the formalist outlook, on this line of thought, is its tendency to treat landscapes as gigantic arrays of lines, shapes and colours when they are actually much more than this. In light of this fundamental flaw, some writers have concluded that Formalism is simply inadequate as a theory of the aesthetics of nature. J.B. Callicott puts the criticism bluntly: 'The prevailing natural aesthetic, therefore, is not autonomous: it does not flow naturally from nature itself; it is not directly oriented to nature on nature's own terms . . . It is superficial and narcissistic. In a word, it is trivial'.[27]

Callicott's remark also suggests a different, although related, objection to Formalism as a theory of the aesthetic appreciation of nature. Recall that, in discussing Formalism's merits, we noted that the formalist can respond to some of the ethical qualms engendered by the postmodernist view. In particular, we noted that the formalist can claim that her view allows one to employ aesthetic value in debates over environmental preservation. But another criticism of the post-modern view was that it is a kind of ethical failing to refuse natural things some degree of respect, to fail to appreciate them 'on their own terms'. The post-modern view is susceptible to this criticism because it essentially endorses the use of natural things as palimpsests for our personal whims and fancies, without regard for 'their own terms'. But Formalism can be tarred with the same brush: to treat, say, a mountain valley as an array of lines, shapes and colours, and nothing more, is also to refuse to consider it on its own terms, for the simple reason that a mountain valley is not an array of lines, shapes and colours, and nothing more. The Formalist approach, in other words, like the post-modern one, manifests a sort of disregard for natural things.

It is also worth noting that these objections to Formalism throw one of the supposed advantages of Formalism, namely the possibility of quantifying aesthetic value, into a quite different light. If, as the critics of Formalism argue, there is more to the aesthetic value of an object than its pure form, then quantification of that form, while it may deliver us a numerical value that is impressive in policy debates, will not be quantification of the object's aesthetic value.[28] To see the force of this point, consider the parallel attempt to quantify the aesthetic value of artworks through a mathematical analysis of their patterns of lines, shapes and colours. While such a project might be engaging, and might tell us some interesting things about artworks, it is doubtful whether this could be taken seriously as an objective measure of their aesthetic value, for the reason that assessing the worth of artworks requires more than the appreciation of pure form. But once again, if this is the case for art, then, in the absence of any good reason to the contrary, the same should hold for the aesthetic appreciation of nature.

This last point may seem deflating, given the inherent attractiveness of resolving debates about the aesthetic quality of nature through some kind of empirical measurement. But we should not despair too quickly, for the notions of 'being resolvable' and 'being resolvable by empirical measurement' are distinct ones. As the example of the aesthetic value of art shows, some issues may not be resolvable by empirical means, but still resolvable. Disputes about the aesthetic value of artworks are often taken to be at least partially resolvable. But this resolution, when we get it, comes from the judgements of art critics, who bring to appreciation an understanding of art history, art theory and particular artworks. By bringing this richer kind of thought component to bear, the critic brings the artwork into focus, allowing a more correct or appropriate aesthetic assessment of its merits. In the case of nature, what figure could play a comparable role? In the next chapter, we will explore one recent, and controversial, answer to this question: the natural scientist.

CHAPTER 4

SCIENCE AND NATURE AESTHETICS

So far, we have examined two important responses to the question 'What kind of thought component is required for appropriate aesthetic appreciation of nature?': (1) any sort at all (the post-modern view) and (2) none, apart from thoughts about perceptual form (Formalism). In this chapter we will examine the first of two approaches that steer a middle course between these extremes, holding that a substantial thought component is needed for appropriate aesthetic appreciation, but rejecting the notion that any and all such components are valid. The approach that we examine in this chapter takes the relevant thought component to be informed by natural science. As we will see, this 'science-based approach' takes us in a very different direction than the previous approaches that we have considered, and raises some new issues about the aesthetics of nature.

SCIENCE AND THE 'NATURE CRITIC'

We can sum up the basic idea behind the science-based approach by saying that appropriate aesthetic appreciation of nature is appreciation with a thought component that is shaped, at least partially, by the body of knowledge about nature compiled by the natural sciences. What this means is that, to appreciate a natural thing appropriately, or, as Hepburn puts it, in a more serious vein, we need to draw upon what science has revealed about that thing: what sort of thing it is, what properties it has, what it does and how it came to be the way that it is.[1]

We can illustrate the view by returning again to our example of appreciating the night sky. In contrast to the defender of the post-modern view, the proponent of the science-based approach would insist that Penny fails to appreciate the night sky appropriately. For although she delights in the look of the stars, her delight emerges from treating them as the outlines of mythological characters, rather than as what they actually are (namely, distant balls of flaming gas that belong to larger astronomical structures such as galaxies). And, in opposition to the formalist, the proponent of the science-based approach view would say something similar about Fred's delight in the pure pattern of the stars, since his thought component also fails to include any of the facts about the stars. For Fred, the stars are merely the elements of a purely formal pattern.

The person who comes closest to appreciating the night sky appropriately, according to the science-based approach, would seem to be Sam, who views the stars as distant bodies separated from us by enormous distances. He may take delight in the striking clarity of the images of the stars, despite their having travelled across such unimaginably large distances. He may also appreciate the view of the various cosmic structures and processes manifest in the pattern of the stars, such as the concentration of many stars, including our sun, in the Milky Way, the intricate movements of the planets, including Earth, due to gravitational forces, the vaporization of comets, and so on.[2] In appreciating the sky in this way, Sam succeeds, to a greater extent than Penny or Fred, in treating the object of appreciation as the natural thing it is, and thus, according to the science-based approach, in appreciating it appropriately. Furthermore, not only does Sam's understanding of what he is looking at in the night sky alter the way the scene appears to him, it also determines what belongs, and what does not belong, to that scene. Sam's knowledge about the stars gives him, as Allen Carlson puts it, 'the appropriate foci of aesthetic significance and the appropriate boundaries of the setting'.[3] For instance, it allows Sam to differentiate between celestial objects and satellites, excluding the latter as parts of the object of his aesthetic appreciation.

Such is the content of the science-based approach: what arguments can be adduced in its favour? Supporters of the science-based approach turn, for support, to two factors that we have already discussed: ethical considerations and the analogy with art argument. Recall that when used in opposition to the post-modern model, the latter argument maintains that serious art criticism does not admit any and all thought components, but neither does it require the purgation of all thought in favour of the savouring of 'pure form'. Rather, serious art criticism requires that the thought component of our appreciation involve the theory and history necessary to understand the artwork. Given the absence of any principled reason why aesthetic appreciation should differ in the case of art, the same ought to hold in that domain. As Carlson puts it:

> If to aesthetically appreciate art we must have knowledge of artistic traditions and styles within those traditions, then to aesthetically

appreciate nature we must have knowledge of the different environments of nature and of the systems and elements within those
environments.[4]

The proponent of the science-based approach will further add that our
chief source of knowledge about nature, though not the exclusive one, is
natural science: the disciplines of natural history, biology, geology,
chemistry, physics, and so on.

On the science-based approach, then, there is a strong analogy between
these disciplines and the disciplines of art history and art theory. In each
case, the relevant disciplines provide facts about the object that serve as
the basis for appropriate aesthetic appraisal of it. But can we press the
analogy further? In Chapter 2, we mentioned that there does not seem to
be a figure who is analogous to the art critic in nature appreciation: there
is no 'nature critic'. The science-based approach, however, makes it
tempting to cast the scientist in this role. Carlson, for example, says that
'in the way in which the art critic and art historian are well equipped to
aesthetically appreciate art, the naturalist and the ecologist are well
equipped to aesthetically appreciate nature'.[5]

It is important to stress the word 'well-equipped' here, though, since
the defender of the science-based approach will not want to say that the
role of scientist is identical to the role of 'nature critic'. Clearly, most
scientific work does not involve aesthetic appreciation of nature at all,
and many, perhaps most scientists, have neither interest in such appreciation nor talent for it. Although science provides us with the understanding
necessary for appropriate nature appreciation, science itself is not a
branch of criticism, and being a good 'nature critic' surely takes more
than having access to this understanding.

Nonetheless, some aesthetically sensitive scientists have occasionally
engaged in nature appreciation, and their writings might be construed as
a form of nature criticism. A notable example is the American naturalist
Aldo Leopold. Leopold clearly took the aesthetic appreciation of nature
seriously: he wrote, for instance, that 'the taste for country displays the
same diversity in aesthetic competence among individuals as the taste for
opera, or oils'.[6] In addition to his scientific work, he wrote essays that
appraise the aesthetic value of nature; in these, he draws on natural
history and science to inform his aesthetic judgements. In these writings,
Leopold appears to be carrying out a role something like that of a 'nature
critic'. Leopold also happened to be a scientist, but this was not essential
for him to play this role. What was essential was that he brought

knowledge, from relevant scientific disciplines, to bear in his appreciation of natural things.

In addition to appealing to the analogy with art, the proponent of the science-based approach will also argue that ethical considerations support her view over its rivals. One such consideration, which some have thought to weigh against the post-modernist and formalist approaches, is the notion that aesthetic appreciation should manifest a respect for nature, a willingness to approach it 'on its own terms'. In the last chapter, we saw some difficulties that Formalism has in meeting this requirement. The prospects of a science-based approach are better here, since, according to such an approach, appropriate aesthetic appreciation requires a thought component that is based on 'the facts' about natural things. Thus Sam's appreciation of the Milky Way as a vast spiral galaxy, rather than the highway of the gods or a bright white strip of light, can be said to display a willingness to approach the starry heavens 'on its own terms'. In this sense it is unlike the appreciation carried out by Fred and Penny, who each fail to take what he or she is appreciating on its own terms, in some fairly significant way. In Penny's case this is done wilfully and deliberately, as when she elects to imagine Callisto in the vault of the stars; in Fred's case it may occur simply because he happened to look up and see a wonderful pattern. But however it occurs, the proponent of the science-based approach will view this failure to see nature for what it is as ethically problematic, and insist that avoiding it is a strength of the science-based approach.

A second ethical consideration that we have considered in evaluating different approaches to nature aesthetics is the ability of an approach to accord aesthetic value a meaningful role in debates regarding environmental preservation. The post-modern view, as you will recall, was faulted on these grounds because it seemingly leaves the aesthetic value of any natural thing or scene a completely subjective matter. There are, on Post-modernism, no more and less correct answers regarding whether a particular natural thing is aesthetically good or bad, since different viewers are free to bring completely different thought components to their appreciation. As Croce put it, even when they disagree completely, conflicting appreciators 'are both right'. But if any assessment at all of the aesthetic value of a natural thing is right, then that value is useless as a basis for deciding how we ought to regard or treat nature. The science-based approach avoids this difficulty, since it holds that all thought components are not equal, with appreciation that is informed by an understanding of nature being more appropriate. Carlson concludes that just as the view that art appreciation requires knowledge from art history and art theory means that the aesthetic value of art is not completely subjective, so the science-based approach means that 'the objectivity of aesthetic judgments about nature is similarly underwritten'.[7]

With regard to this issue, however, it may still appear that Formalism has an advantage over the science-based approach. For according to Formalism, the aesthetic character of a natural thing can be seen, not only as objective, but also as quantifiable. That is, if Formalism is correct, not only can we say that there are more and less correct answers regarding how aesthetically appealing a particular landscape is, we can actually put a number on its aesthetic value. The proponent of the science-based approach will concede that her view is unable to match this feat. But she will also insist that being able to a put a number on the aesthetic value of a landscape is of no value if what that number measures is not the aesthetic value of the natural entity in question. And in formal appreciation, this is exactly the case: in such appreciation, we quantify features of an array of lines, shapes and colours but not the aesthetic value of a mountain valley. On the science-based approach, the aesthetic value of a natural area has to be judged by an agent able to deploy the right thought component and possessed of the various other capacities needed in aesthetic judgement – in other words, a good 'nature critic'. The mind-set prevailing in many environmental policy debates can make it tempting to reach for a number – any number – to pin on the aesthetic value of nature. Without it, aesthetic value may be simply dismissed in favour of more readily quantifiable considerations. But it is in the nature of some things to elude quantification: such things simply call for considered, informed judgement. If the judgements of art critics are able to resolve, at least in some cases, questions regarding the aesthetic value of artworks, we ought to expect no less in the case of natural things.

A final ethical consideration from which proponents of the science-based approach can draw support for their view is the impact of the view on our actual treatment of nature. Here they maintain that, in contrast to the post-modernist and formalist approaches, their view will lead to less mistreatment and mismanagement of nature on our part, and to better outcomes for natural things. One strand of this reasoning has to do with the assumptions about nature that are involved in the post-modernist and formalist approaches. Consider again Eaton's discussion of *Bambi*. According to Eaton, the *Bambi*-inspired conception of deer has led to negative outcomes for the environment by making it more difficult to take certain measures needed to manage deer populations. In other cases, overly imaginative conceptions of animals have engendered myths and misapprehensions about them, leading people to view and treat them negatively. Consider the way in which the treatment of snakes and sharks has been affected by consistent depiction of these creatures in a generally negative light.[8] The proponent of the science-based approach will insist that we can go a good way towards avoiding these sorts of problems by rejecting post-modernist and formalist views and insisting that our aesthetic appreciation 'be based upon, tempered by, directed and enriched by solid ecological knowledge'.[9]

There is also another strand to the view that the science-based approach will lead to a better treatment of nature, which is the thought that it will expand the scope of what we find aesthetically appealing in nature. To appreciate this point fully, we need to explore further the implications of the science-based approach for the aesthetic value of nature. According to some, its ramifications are nothing short of revolutionary.

ANOTHER TURN IN THE TASTE FOR LANDSCAPE?

In Chapter 1, we saw how the eighteenth century witnessed a remarkable broadening of taste in natural scenery. As the concepts of the picturesque and the sublime developed and gained acceptance in European culture, landscapes that had previously been viewed with disgust or fear became objects of aesthetic appreciation. Ancient prejudices about mountains, for example, were put aside as people learned to take aesthetic delight in the varied appearances of nature. The eighteenth century's 'revolution' in the taste for landscape, however, only extended so far. Mountains, raging waterfalls and picturesque scenery became widely appreciated, but other sorts of landscape, such as the wetland and the prairie, did not. As Neil Evernden notes, even today surveys of landscape preference find that prairie scenes are 'invariably rated esthetically poor, even by those who [have] grown up on the prairie'.[10] This exclusion of certain landscapes from contemporary taste was noted by Leopold, who wrote that 'There are those who are willing to be herded in droves through "scenic" places; who find mountains grand if they be proper mountains with waterfalls, cliffs, and lakes. To such the Kansas plains are tedious'.[11] As for wetlands, Holmes Rolston goes so far as to suggest that, in our minds, these places 'have "ugliness" built into them': phrases like 'beautiful bog' and 'pleasant mire' are, he notes, 'almost a contradiction in terms'.[12] The upshot of the eighteenth century's broadening of our taste for landscape, then, is a division in natural scenery that persists to this day: the division between what we regard as the 'scenic masterpieces', such as mountains, and the plain, or even ugly, environments that Yuriko Saito calls 'scenically challenged'.[13]

Proponents of the science-based approach have argued that this division has been a harmful one, in that it has led to a relative devaluing of the scenically challenged landscapes. When decisions about the preservation of natural areas are made, scenically challenged environments are at a disadvantage owing to their homeliness. For instance, when the creation of Florida Everglades national park was first proposed in the 1930s, the conservationist William T. Hornaday objected, noting that in the Everglades, he had 'found mighty little that was of special interest, and absolutely nothing that was picturesque or beautiful'. Hornaday conceded that 'the saw-grass Everglades Swamp is not as ugly and repulsive as some other swamps that I have seen', but insisted that 'it is yet a *long ways* from being fit to elevate into a national park, to put alongside the magnificent array of scenic wonderlands that the American people have elevated into that glorious class.'[14] Summing up the view of the prairie landscape that emerged from early empirical landscape assessment studies, Evernden writes that

> from the point of view of an official charged with ensuring that the most valuable visual resources are preserved, the prairie could be ignored. Any use of prairie would be acceptable, because no one cares about viewing the prairie. The public has ruled prairie beauty nonexistent.[15]

Some have argued, however, that this narrowness of vision regarding what counts as a 'scenic wonderland' is, in fact, a failing in our aesthetic judgement. In particular, some defenders of the science-based approach have suggested that this narrowness is the product of our adopting misleading approaches to the aesthetics of nature, such as Formalism and the post-modern view. Formalism, for instance, leads us to think of aesthetic value in terms of certain appealing arrays of lines, shapes and colours. We find these in certain landscapes, such as great mountain ranges, but when confronted with the vast emptiness of a prairie landscape, they are absent.[16] Post-modernism, on the other hand, encourages us to bring our own ideas, values and associations to nature; as Croce puts it, it is ourselves we see in nature. But small wonder, then, that it is high mountains and roaring cataracts that we find attractive, rather than wetlands!

Both these approaches leave little room for aesthetic qualities in these sorts of landscape. But once we move beyond these approaches to the science-based approach, this line of thought goes, we will see that our dismissal of aesthetic value in the plain and the wetland was overly hasty, since, when appreciated in light of natural science, these environments too can appear aesthetically pleasing. The idea here is that, just as mountains became aesthetically attractive after we rejected superstitious prejudices and saw them for what they are, so will scenically challenged environments become pleasing, when we come to see them for what they are.

Consider the prairie landscape, for instance. To the casual glance, the prairie appears 'tedious', as Leopold put it, for the sensible enough reason that there is, quite literally, nothing to look at in it, excepting (if one is lucky) some interesting clouds and, of course, the ubiquitous flat horizon. The prairie view is, rather, simply a void. But rumination on the natural history of the prairie landscape may alter this perception. Leopold complained that the tourists 'look at the low horizon, but they cannot see it, as de Vaca did, under the bellies of the buffalo.'[17] To see the prairies 'under the bellies of the buffalo', perhaps, is to see it as a specialized habitat for a wide range of creatures, each adapted to thrive in its particular climate and terrain.[18] Reflection on natural history might even bring the boring, monotonous flatness of the prairie itself to life, causing it to appear stark and striking – as Candace Savage nicely puts it, 'spectacularly featureless'.[19] For after all, its flatness *is* a marvel, the product of flattening by massive glaciers grinding it down over thousands of years. The flatness of the prairie does not seem at all unusual when we think of it in comparison with highly artificial terrain, such as the suburban lawn or the golf course, but in nature its flatness is profoundly distinctive. Finally, the whole prairie scene might take on a different cast when one remembers that those glaciers melted into vast seas that, not so very long ago, covered the entire landscape, making these presently land-locked grasslands an ancient seabed. As Ronald Hepburn puts it in discussing a slightly different example, this realization might make the entire scene take on a slightly eerie quality.[20]

In the case of wetlands, J.B. Callicott argues that wetlands cease to look merely hideous and foul when we approach them with an awareness of the ecological relationships that their components bear to one another, and to other parts of the environment. To a first glance, wetlands seem disordered: mere clumps of moss and tangles of grass, with insects and birds randomly arranged, and the whole thing drenched in fetid and mucky standing water. Yet an understanding of the ecological relations between these various elements may change the way we perceive them and their relations. Callicott writes:

> The sphagnum moss and the chemical regime it imposes constitutes [*sic*] the basis of this small, tight community. The tamaracks are a second major factor. The flora and fauna of the stories between are characteristic of, and some like the pitcher plants are unique to, this sort of community. There is a sensible fittingness, a unity there, not unlike that of a good symphony or tragedy.[21]

The basic idea, then, is that the acceptance of the science-based approach entails a further expansion in the aesthetic taste for landscape, beyond that seen in the eighteenth century. For even when there is, apparently, not much to look at, an understanding of science and natural history can make what little there is pleasing to behold.[22] The scope of this change, however, is potentially much wider than that of its eighteenth-century predecessor. According to some proponents of the science-based approach, *absolutely everything* in nature takes on significant aesthetic value, when seen in light of scientific information about it. This view, the view that all natural things have positive aesthetic value, is generally referred to as 'Positive Aesthetics' for nature. Proponents of the science-based view see this as an advantage of their view, insofar as Positive Aesthetics promises to make aesthetic preservation possible for hitherto scenically challenged landscapes.

However, Positive Aesthetics for nature is a controversial view. First, note that the view is intuitively implausible. We can see this by considering a parallel claim of Positive Aesthetics for art. Such a claim would hold that absolutely all artworks, when properly appreciated, have some significant level of aesthetic goodness: there are no aesthetically poor artworks. Even a cursory glance at the art of any given period confirms that this is not the case: much art is mediocre, and some of it is truly awful. What reason, then, do proponents of the science-based approach give for accepting such a counter-intuitive view, when it comes to nature?

We will briefly examine two recent arguments for the claim that Positive Aesthetics for nature (hereafter simply 'Positive Aesthetics') follows from the science-based approach to nature appreciation. Each of these arguments develops, in a different way, the idea that conceptualizing nature in terms of the information provided by natural science always leads to our finding a significant amount of aesthetic value in the perceptual appearance of nature. The first argument is due to Yuriko Saito, who argues that natural science demonstrates that every thing in nature has an interesting story: whether it is an organism, a rock, a lake or a cloud, some branch of natural science discloses a rich account of how that natural thing came to be, how it works and what it is composed of. Further, Saito argues that these stories are *'presented* in the visual composition' of natural things; consequently, knowing those interesting stories causes their visual composition to appear differently. As she puts it:

> While there may be different degrees of nature's skill in storytelling, none of its parts are mute. Simply by virtue of exhibiting various perceptual features, they all bear witness to their own origin, structure, and function, which we articulate verbally in our scientific accounts.[23]

In the case of the prairie landscape, for example, even though there are few visual elements to appreciate, these elements 'bear witness to', or 'reveal' interesting stories about the landscape. Thus the flatness of the prairie is not the mundane flatness of the suburban lawn: it is a palpable glimpse of an ancient geological process operating on an almost unimaginable scale. Positive Aesthetics for nature holds true, on Saito's line of thought, because nature's perceptual form is never 'mute': it everywhere reveals some such process that, for those who can 'read nature's story', give it aesthetic interest.

A somewhat different argument in favour of Positive Aesthetics is offered by Allen Carlson. Unlike Saito's, Carlson's argument is based on a particular feature of scientific accounts of natural phenomena. As he puts it,

> A more correct categorization in science is one that over time makes the natural world seem more intelligible, more comprehensible to those whose science it is. Our science appeals to certain kinds of qualities to accomplish this. These qualities are ones such as order, regularity, harmony, balance, tension, resolution, and so forth . . . These qualities that make the world seem comprehensible to us are also those that we find aesthetically good. Thus, when we experience them in the natural world or experience the natural world in terms of them, we find it aesthetically good.[24]

On Carlson's view, then, it is no surprise that appreciation that is informed by scientific accounts of nature, as per the science-based approach, would lead to Positive Aesthetics. Scientific accounts are, by definition, those that render nature intelligible. But they cannot render nature intelligible without also exposing some order, regularity and pattern in it. This order, regularity and pattern then can serve, not only to facilitate intelligibility, but to facilitate aesthetic appreciation as well. We can also see why, on Carlson's reasoning, an alternative view such as Formalism does not lead to Positive Aesthetics. According to Formalism, things are aesthetically good when they possess certain configurations of lines, shapes and colours, and it is certainly possible for a particular natural thing to lack those particular configurations. But if Carlson's reasoning is correct, it is not possible for a natural thing to be aesthetically appreciated in light of its scientific categorization and yet lack aesthetic value, for that very categorization endows it, indeed must endow it, with the aesthetic qualities of order, regularity and harmony.

Other philosophers sympathetic to the science-based approach have offered different arguments for Positive Aesthetics, and the attraction to the claim is not difficult to fathom. If Positive Aesthetics is true, then the ethical considerations favouring the science-based approach will be even more forceful. Not only will adopting the science-based approach ensure a more respectful attitude to nature, and result in less sentimental or fanciful misrepresentation of it, it will also engender a more egalitarian approach to Aesthetic Preservation. Aesthetic value will no longer only apply to the scenic wonders, such as mountains, but to all nature. Hence it will be more useful in attempts to preserve traditionally neglected natural areas: environmentalists will be able to argue for the preservation of prairie landscapes and wetlands, for instance, on aesthetic, as well practical, grounds.

OBJECTIONS TO THE SCIENCE-BASED APPROACH

Philosophers have advanced a wide variety of objections to the science-based approach. Some of these are perhaps best described as objections to certain implications of the approach. For example, some have noted that a science-based approach would entail that some, perhaps much, actual aesthetic appreciation of nature is less appropriate, or even inappropriate appreciation. Stephanie Ross, discussing scientific knowledge about the autumn changes in leaf colours, brings out this point by observing that if such knowledge is required for appropriate aesthetic appreciation, then 'I have never *truly* appreciated the New England woods that I have walked through in any of the four seasons.'[25] Others have charged that the view is elitist, in holding that the naturalist and the ecologist are better equipped to aesthetically appreciate nature than those of us who lack their insight into the workings of nature. Emily Brady, for example, notes that the science-based approach imposes 'intellectual demands' on appreciators, and worries that these demands 'potentially disqualify [some] accounts of aesthetic experiences in the deliberative process because they are not grounded in sufficient knowledge'.[26] And still others find the view to impart to nature an aesthetic character that is too fixed and static, constraining our freedom in interpreting and conceptualizing nature, and ultimately limiting our enjoyment.[27]

Each of these objections seizes on a state of affairs that indeed is entailed by the science-based approach. However, none of them provides much basis for rejecting the science-based approach, since none of the objections call into question either the ethical considerations or the analogy with art that support the view. On the contrary, the defender of the science-based view will claim that when we take these factors into account, the states of affairs on which these objections are founded can appear rather unremarkable. For instance, the proponent of the science-based approach can point out that each of these states of affairs, in fact, is widely thought to obtain in the case of art appreciation. Much of the art appreciation that people carry out – casually strolling through an art gallery and picking out the pieces that happen to strike one's eye, for example – is not exactly serious appreciation. Generally, we take those who have studied art theory and art history to be better qualified than the casual gallery stroller to judge the aesthetic achievement of particular artworks – in that sense, art appreciation is 'elitist', but elitism so construed is not objectionable but entirely sensible. It seems reasonable, for example, that galleries are run, and art competitions adjudicated, by those with the knowledge and experience required to understand and assess particular artworks. And finally, no one takes the fact that we might wring more enjoyment out of an artwork by inventing a fictitious author for it, or by considering it as something it patently is not, such as a work from a different period, as sufficient grounds for admitting such practices in serious art criticism. In sum, since all of these supposedly objectionable states of affairs hold in art, the fact that they also hold in nature does not seem to raise any special difficulty for the science-based approach.

A more persuasive objection would strike at one of the sources of justification for the view: the analogy with art argument itself. One such objection is the charge that there is an important difference between scientific knowledge and knowledge from art history and art theory. The latter sort of knowledge seems capable, at least in many cases, of playing a role in actually altering our aesthetic responses to art. An understanding of the genre of cubism – a grasp of its conventions for using particular shapes and for depicting movement, for instance – does seem to influence what we see in cubist paintings. When we learn what cubist artists are doing, an elegant arrangement can emerge in what may have initially seemed a hopeless jumble of random shapes. But in the case of scientific knowledge, one might worry whether such knowledge can actually alter what we see in the same manner. Scientific knowledge is, by its nature, somewhat abstract and theoretical. When we think in terms of scientific principles and laws, we often lose contact with the particular objects that we can perceive with our senses. In this sense, scientific knowledge may seem more likely to be a hindrance or an obstruction to the aesthetic appreciation of nature than to be a source of enrichment for it.

This worry has a long history. In the nineteenth-century Romantic Movement, poets such as William Wordsworth and William Blake expressed discomfort with overly intellectual approaches to nature. Wordsworth famously wrote of the 'meddling intellect' that 'Mis-shapes the beauteous forms of things'.[28] But unease with science is not found only in Romantic literature. Mark Twain, in his memoir *Life on the Mississippi*, remarked on the effect that learning the scientific principles of steamboat navigation had on his appreciation of the river: 'the romance and the beauty were all gone from the river. All the value any feature of it had for me now was the amount of usefulness it could furnish towards compassing the safe piloting of a steamboat.'[29] Echoing Twain's remarks, Thomas Heyd suggests that the science-based approach may also lead aesthetic appreciation astray:

> . . . if my cognizance of geology, chemistry, or botany were to lead me to really focus on, for example, seeking appropriate scientific classifications for the Olympic mountains, the watery expanse, or the arbutus tree I sit beneath, diverting my attention from the natural objects and sites concretely at hand, such knowledge should be considered harmful to my aesthetic appreciation of the natural environment in which I am immersed.[30]

Along the same lines, Ronald Hepburn notes that some thought components are so abstract and theoretical that they 'fragment or overwhelm
or dissolve the aesthetic perception, instead of enriching it'.[31] When a
thought component is of this kind, he argues, we can be under no obligation to employ it, for to do so is to destroy, rather than enrich, aesthetic
appreciation. In short, the worry behind this objection is that the science-
based approach turns out not to be a theory of the *aesthetic* appreciation
of nature at all: on the contrary, to approach nature in this way is to think
of it scientifically, shifting our attention away from the perceptual appearance of nature, and so away from nature's aesthetic qualities.

In response to this objection, defenders of the science-based approach
typically point out that natural science contains a wide range of different
kinds of knowledge, from the sort of information provided by the abstract
mathematical laws of physics to the particularized histories of specific
ecosystems and organisms that we find in evolutionary biology and natural history. The defender of science-based approach can hold that, even if
knowledge from the more abstract and general end of this spectrum fails
to enhance, or even interferes with, aesthetic appreciation, knowledge
from the other end of the spectrum can enhance it. Saito, for example,
writes that

> We have to concede that indeed *some* scientific information does
> lead us away from the actual experience of nature. For example, the
> molecular structure of a rock or the medicinal value of a spring
> seems too removed from our immediate perceptual arena to be real-
> izable on the sensuous surface. In general . . . aesthetically irrelevant
> considerations belong to early modern sciences within the rational-
> ist tradition (such as physics and chemistry) . . . On the other hand,
> some other scientific information enhances or modifies our initial
> perceptual experience of nature. Such information is derived from
> . . . the natural history sciences (such as geology and biology) . . .[32]

Thus, in our example of appreciating the night sky, the knowledge that is
said to be capable of enriching appreciation might involve things like the
size, position and behaviour of stars, but perhaps not the laws governing
the subatomic reactions occurring inside them. And in the case of appreciating a prairie landscape, descriptions of the geological processes that
shaped the land may enhance our appreciation, whereas descriptions of
soil composition do not. The former descriptions, in each case, seem to
be, as Saito puts it, 'realizable on the sensuous surface', in that including

them in the thought component of our appreciation does seem capable of changing the object's aesthetic qualities.

In advancing this response, the proponent of the science-based approach can again point to the analogy with art for support, for the same point holds, though to a lesser degree, regarding the appreciation of art. Some historical information about artworks can enrich our aesthetic appreciation, but some does not. Knowing the political context in which the work was created, for example, might enrich our aesthetic appreciation of it, but knowing, say, how many owners it has had typically does not. In nature appreciation, there is always the danger of becoming so caught up in information about the object that one simply ceases to aesthetically appreciate the object at all. But this is a danger for any sort of aesthetic appreciation, including the appreciation of art.

Even if this response is compelling, however, the ethical considerations that have been adduced in support of the science-based approach have also been challenged. As we have seen, proponents of the science-based approach claim that their approach to nature appreciation is apt to result in a more ethical treatment of nature since we generally treat nature better when our engagement with it is 'based upon, tempered by, directed and enriched by solid ecological knowledge', as Marcia Eaton puts it. But some philosophers, including some environmental philosophers, are sceptical of this claim. Ned Hettinger, for example, has suggested that, on the contrary, 'aesthetic responses based on ecological ignorance and myth may sometimes be the best for aesthetic protectionism'.[33] In support of his suggestion, Hettinger points to the view, once orthodoxy in ecology, that nature possesses an ideal balanced state that we ought to try to maintain. This view, as he notes, has largely been discredited within the science of ecology, in favour of the view that ecosystems are dynamic and continually in flux.[34] But from the standpoint of encouraging a less exploitative attitude towards the environment, this falsehood may well be superior to the truth. One might also support Hettinger's suggestion by pointing to certain indigenous cultures that approach nature primarily, if not exclusively, through the lens of traditional myths and creation stories that encourage a harmonious relationship with the environment.

Critics have also challenged the claim that the science-based approach will encourage a better ethical relationship to nature by greatly expanding our conception of what is aesthetically good in nature. In particular, philosophers have questioned some of the arguments for Positive Aesthetics presented by defenders of the science-based approach. Consider again Saito's argument for the claim. According to that line of thought, everything in nature is aesthetically good since the perceptual appearance of everything in nature expresses or bears witness to its history or ecological role in some way. But is it really true that everything in nature expresses or bears witness to its history or its ecological role? Certainly some things in nature possess perceptual appearances that 'speak' of their origin and place in nature. For example, consider the sensory appearance produced by a stratified rock face. The visual pattern that the rock presents has a certain resemblance to its geological history. In a very concrete sense, we can 'see' geological history when we look at the rock itself, and we may well enjoy the rock aesthetically in light of this. But surely not every natural thing speaks of its history or place in nature in this way: a rock formation that is a uniformly coloured surface and the surface of a large body of water, for instance, do not seem to do so. Although these objects may be the subject of interesting stories, they do not seem to *present* those stories in their visual composition.[35]

Carlson's argument for Positive Aesthetics has also been criticized. His argument turns on the idea that good scientific descriptions and accounts necessarily render the things that they describe more intelligible. Carlson claims that, in doing so, they cause those things to appear more orderly, regular and harmonious, and thus aesthetically good. Malcolm Budd objects that the fact that scientific theories, by definition, render natural phenomena understandable, and thus to some extent, orderly, regular and harmonious, does not mean that those theories will make nature look aesthetically good. Budd gives the example of 'grossly malformed living things', which, he argues, 'remain grotesque no matter how comprehensible science renders their malformation'.[36]

As a different example, consider the phenomenon of elephant stampeding. If we are to understand it scientifically, this phenomenon must exhibit order, in some sense. It must occur in response to certain environmental stimuli or internal cues with some regularity (i.e. in some more or less predictable way). If it did not, it would be purely random and inexplicable. But it hardly follows that, just because a scientific theory allows us to understand it, elephant stampeding *looks* orderly or harmonious. The predicate 'orderly' applies primarily to the entire historical sequence of events involved in elephant stampeding: this sequence is orderly in the sense that we can identify, in this sequence, cause and effect. But it is not such sequences upon which we pass aesthetic judgement: it is rather the sight of a herd of stampeding elephants. Carlson's argument for Positive Aesthetics for nature fails, in other words, because the orderliness that understanding a thing scientifically entails often simply fails to translate into the perceptual appearance of that thing. In the absence of a compelling argument for it, Positive Aesthetics has seemed to some to be, rather than an accurate description of the aesthetic character of nature as a whole, a 'politically correct' prohibition against pointing out the ugliness of certain natural things – as Terry Diffey has put it, a 'sentimental a priori thought'.[37]

If the reasoning pursued above is on the right track, then the ethical considerations supporting the science-based approach are weaker than some have suggested. For all that, however, the proponent of this approach might still appeal to the ethical argument involving respect for nature, as well as the analogy with art argument, to support her view over its rivals, Formalism and Post-modernism. In the next chapter, we will examine the claim that, properly understood, these arguments do not lead us to a science-based approach at all, but rather to a pluralistic aesthetics of nature.

CHAPTER 5

PLURALISM

In this chapter, we consider a pluralist approach to the aesthetics of nature.[1] Proponents of this view, like defenders of the science-based approach discussed in Chapter 4, reject Formalism and Post-modernism as inadequate frameworks for thinking about the aesthetic qualities of natural things. However, the pluralist also insists that the science-based approach represents an overreaction to the flaws of these frameworks. Accordingly, the pluralist rejects the notion that the aesthetic appreciation of nature must be informed by natural science. Rather, the pluralist endorses a wide range of different ways of aesthetically appreciating nature. In our discussion, we will distinguish between two different versions of the pluralist position, based on two different views as to the extent of this range, considering the merits of each.

MODERATE PLURALISM

At the end of the previous chapter, we noted two chief arguments offered in support of the science-based approach. The first, the analogy with art argument, holds that we ought to think about the aesthetic appreciation of nature along the same general lines as we think about the aesthetic appreciation of art, unless there is some principled reason to do otherwise. Since aesthetically appreciating an artwork appropriately requires knowing pertinent facts about it from the disciplines of art history and art theory, we ought to hold that the appreciation of nature also requires knowledge of some facts about the object of appreciation, facts to be provided by the analogous discipline of natural science. The second chief argument in favour of the science-based approach is an ethical one. On this argument, appropriate aesthetic appreciation of nature should not involve the adoption of an ethically problematic attitude, such as showing disrespect for nature. Given that we must recognize nature as what it actually is in order to show respect for it, the proponent of the science-based approach again concludes that appropriate aesthetic appreciation of nature requires employing knowledge from the natural sciences.

The pluralist rejects these as arguments in favour of the science-based approach. However, her view is not that they are entirely misguided. The pluralist can accept the truth of some of the premises in these arguments, for example. Further, she can accept that arguments along these lines suffice to demonstrate the inadequacy of post-modern and formalist approaches to appreciating nature. The pluralist's criticism is that proponents of the science-based approach have mishandled these arguments, drawing erroneous and somewhat overblown conclusions from some true premises. When properly understood, these arguments actually support a pluralist, not a purely science-based, approach. More specifically, the pluralist claims that these arguments allow us to include, as forms of appropriate aesthetic appreciation, not only scientifically informed appreciation, but also certain kinds of formal appreciation, and what one philosopher calls 'being moved by nature'.

Let us first consider why the pluralist thinks that the analogy with art argument also licences these various forms of appreciation. The pluralist can accept the main premise of the analogy with art argument: namely, we ought to think about the appreciation of nature along the same general lines as we think about the appreciation of art, unless there is some principled reason to do otherwise. Furthermore, she can accept the premise that in art appreciation, not all thought components are permissible: some ways of conceiving of the work produce inappropriate appreciation. But she will insist that these points do not show that knowing facts about a particular artwork, from art history and art theory, is, strictly speaking, necessary for appropriate aesthetic appreciation of that work. Sometimes, we can aesthetically appreciate artworks appropriately without bringing any such knowledge to bear.

The first way this can be done is in formal appreciation of the artwork: attention to its pure arrangement of lines, shapes and colours. In discussing criticisms of Formalism, we noted that if we view an artwork in terms of its pure form alone, we will miss many of its aesthetic qualities, and come away with a distorted sense of its aesthetic achievement. For example, if we appreciate a work such as Raphael's famous *Galatea* (1513) fresco solely in terms of its lines, shapes and colours, we are missing much of what it has to offer aesthetically. But this does not mean that appreciating a work apart from knowledge about its genre and history is *always*, or in every instance, inappropriate. One might delight in the harmonious juxtaposition of colours in *Galatea*, for example, without knowing anything about the work's genre, or anything about the art historical developments of which it is a part. One is simply struck by the harmony of the colour arrangement. If this is the *only* way in which we approach the work, of course, we will miss many of its other aesthetic qualities, including those for which knowledge of certain facts about the work's genre and art historical context is required. But it doesn't follow from this that we need to know such facts in order to appreciate *any* of its aesthetic qualities. Some of these qualities are simply apparent to us, even in the absence of such knowledge.

If this line of thought about the aesthetic appreciation of art is correct, then the analogy with art argument ought to lead us to see formal appreciation of nature as also perfectly appropriate, when viewed as a way of appreciating *some* of the object's aesthetic qualities. Critics of Formalism in the aesthetics of nature, as we have seen, charge that to appreciate nature simply as an array of lines, shapes and colours is to fail to appreciate nature as what it is. But although nature is more than a perceptual array of lines, shapes and colours, such a perceptual array is a part of what nature is. Donald Crawford expresses this point by saying that 'what we can experience when we adopt the painter's eye in viewing nature' is '*the effects of nature* on us as perceivers'.[2] The rock face of a cliff, for instance, being the sort of thing that it is, produces a certain sort of perceptual impression in us, a certain sort of visual pattern. When we appreciate the rock face simply in virtue of this impression, we are appreciating it as the natural thing that it is – namely, a thing that produces this kind of perceptual impression – even though we are not, at that moment, appreciating *all* of the aspects that it has as the natural thing that it is. At that moment, we do not appreciate its geological history, or its role as a habitat for living creatures, for example.

We also considered a different, though related, criticism of Formalism – the charge that it tends to lead us to disengage ourselves physically from nature. In order to take in the forest as a set of lines, shapes and colours, the formalist needs to withdraw to a distance that allows her to best compose the scene. But in doing so, she winds up with an impoverished appreciation of the forest, missing many of the aesthetic aspects of the things it contains, and losing altogether the sense of envelopment that the forest brings. The pluralist can concede that this sort of 'disengaged' appreciation causes us to miss much of what nature has to offer, but for the pluralist, this is not a difficulty, since she sees such formal appreciation as only one dimension of the appreciation of nature. Ira Newman points out that when we appreciate a natural environment, disengaged formal appreciation is often just one phase in our appreciation:

Sometimes natural settings really are *before us* and out of our reach – at least for the time being. But then we advance further in our walk and our scene is metamorphosed into a perceptual field where the viewing distance is diminished. Environmental circumstances are rich enough to present both the distant panorama plus that which is contiguous to us and palpable.[3]

If we were to appreciate nature only from the roadside turnout, and never become immersed in it, this would surely be a deficient form of appreciation. But pursued as one part of a richer, pluralist approach, there seems nothing objectionable about such appreciation.

In addition to formal appreciation, the pluralist can also claim that other perfectly appropriate ways of aesthetically appreciating nature are left out of the science-based approach. One such form of appreciation has been documented by Noël Carroll. In his discussion of the aesthetic appreciation of nature, Carroll emphasizes occasions on which we are, as he puts it, 'moved emotionally by nature'. As examples, he gives a moment where we find ourselves 'standing under a thundering waterfall . . . excited by its grandeur' or when 'standing barefooted amidst a silent arbor, softly carpeted with layers of decaying leaves, a sense of repose and homeyness [is] aroused in us'.[4] This is, Carroll points out, a kind of aesthetic appreciation of nature: we do not only feel excited, or experience a sense of repose, but also delight in the way nature's appearance is connected with, and reflective of, those feelings. In the case of the waterfall, for example, we fix our gaze on certain aspects of that natural object: the 'palpable force of the cascade, its height, the volume of water, the way it alters the surrounding atmosphere, etc.'[5]

This sort of appreciation involves a thought component on our part, in that we conceptualize the natural object when we have the emotional response that we do. For example, in order to be moved by the grandeur of something, such as a waterfall, we need to conceptualize it as a large object. In this regard, the sort of aesthetic response to nature that Carroll describes is not a formalist one.[6] But unlike the scientifically informed sort of appreciation described in the science-based approach, this brand of appreciation does not require any specialized knowledge of nature at all. Being moved by the grandeur of a waterfall, as Carroll puts it

only requires being human, equipped with the senses we have, being small, and able to intuit the immense force, relative to creatures like us, of the roaring tons of water. Nor need the common sense of our culture come into play. Conceivably humans from other planets bereft of waterfalls could share our sense of grandeur.[7]

Being moved by nature is, in other words, though not a formalist sort of appreciation, closer to formalism than it is to the scientifically informed appreciation of the science-based approach. For the thought content it involves is of a garden variety sort, the kind of conceptualization that any normal person with properly functioning perceptual faculties would instinctively bring to nature. Carroll himself calls being moved by nature a 'more naïve' kind of appreciation, and describes it as 'less intellective, more visceral'.[8]

However, Carroll argues, this sort of appreciation is just as appropriate as scientifically informed appreciation. Consider again the analogy with art argument. This argument compels us to appreciate nature as what it is, rather than something it is not. But when we are moved by nature, we respond to the way nature is, as nature: to creatures like us, a waterfall *is* large, fast and powerful. The same sort of response occurs, as Carroll points out, with artworks. He writes:

> Sometimes we may be emotionally aroused – indeed, appropriately emotionally moved – without knowing the genre or style of the art-work that induces this state. Think of children amused by capers of *commedia dell'arte* but who know nothing of its tradition or its place among other artistic genres, styles and categories.[9]

Presumably, when children are amused by the capers in *commedia dell'arte* it is because they take them to be silly and funny. But they *are* silly and funny, so that the children who are so amused are appreciating the work for what it is. Of course, they do not consider all of the work's different aspects, and so do not appreciate many of its other aesthetic qualities, but for all that they still perceive some of them. According to Carroll, we ought to remember that being moved by an artwork does not give us access to all of a work's aesthetic qualities, but there is no reason to think that such appreciation is in any way inappropriate or defective. Given these facts about art appreciation, Carroll asks, 'Why presume that there is only one model for appreciating nature and one source of knowledge – such as natural history – relevant to fixing our appreciative categories?'[10]

This reasoning can also be extended to the second chief argument offered in support of the science-based approach, the ethical argument. According to the proponent of the science-based approach, appropriate aesthetic appreciation of nature ought not to manifest an ethically problematic attitude, such as disrespect, towards nature. Rather, in aesthetically appreciating nature we ought to 'take it on its own terms'. The pluralist can accept this premise, but she will disagree as to what exactly constitutes adopting an attitude of respect for nature, or taking nature on its own terms. The pluralist might agree with the proponent of the science-based approach that imagining a pair of mountains to be a gigantic set of breasts, or pretending that a wild animal has human-like intentions and aims, entails disrespect for nature and fails to take it on its own terms. But these are cases where natural things are treated, in a cavalier fashion, as being something they are not. Appreciating nature for its formal aesthetic qualities, or in terms of the way that its appearance moves us emotionally, however, are not cases of this kind. If we simply appreciate the array of lines, shapes and colours in a rock face, or the moving grandeur of a waterfall, we neither treat nature in a cavalier way, nor construe it as something it is not. Consequently, the pluralist will argue that to appreciate natural things in these ways is not to show disrespect for it, or fail to take it on its own terms. So once again, an argument that was thought to lead us to a rigidly science-based approach in fact leads us to a pluralistic conception of the aesthetics of nature.

This is not to say that scientifically informed appreciation has no place in the pluralist's conception of the aesthetics of nature: on the contrary, this kind of appreciation is perfectly appropriate on the pluralist's view. Seeing the stars in terms of astronomical facts and information, appreciating a wetland in virtue of the ecological relationships of its components and delighting in the geological sculpting of a prairie landscape all count as legitimate forms of aesthetic appreciation, on the pluralist's conception. Accordingly, the pluralist will heartily recommend that we learn about and deploy information from the natural sciences in our aesthetic appreciation of nature. But she will also remind us that we are under no onus to employ it, and that science-based appreciation does not possess any special or privileged place in the aesthetics of nature, as asserted by boosters of the science-based approach. On the pluralist's view, there just is nothing that makes a scientifically informed appreciation of the night sky, for instance, any better than, say, a formalist appreciation, *as aesthetic appreciation of the stars*. We may employ scientific understanding, if we feel like it, but the quality or appropriateness of our aesthetic judgements about nature does not suffer for our choosing not to do so.

ROBUST PLURALISM

In the previous section, we considered a pluralist approach that admits at least three equally appropriate forms of aesthetic appreciation of nature: scientifically informed appreciation, formal appreciation and being moved by nature. That view, however, still rules out many other sorts of appreciation as inappropriate, including cases where natural things are viewed as things they are not. In this section, we will consider a more robust, wide-ranging Pluralism, which admits even cases of this kind. Considering this view will take us almost full circle, to a position close, though not identical, to the post-modernist view with which we began in Chapter 2.

Like the more moderate variety discussed in the previous section, the more robust brand of Pluralism emerges from a reconsideration of the arguments used to support the science-based approach: namely, the analogy with art argument and the ethical argument. The robust pluralist makes two important claims about these arguments. The first is that these two arguments boil down, ultimately, to the same idea. Consider first the analogy with art argument. The robust pluralist will accept the argument's underlying premise that we ought to think about the aesthetic appreciation of nature along the same general lines as we think about the aesthetic appreciation of art, unless there is some principled reason to do otherwise. Furthermore, he will accept the premise that in art appreciation, not all thought components are permissible: some produce inappropriate appreciation. However, he will insist that the only ground for discounting certain thought components as inappropriate, in the appreciation of art, is an ethical one: namely, that employing them is a way of disrespecting the artwork, of failing to take it 'on its own terms'. Along these lines, Yuriko Saito writes that

Our refusal to experience an art object on its own terms, that is, within its own historical and cultural context as well as by reference to the artist's intention, indicates our unwillingness to put aside (at least to a certain extent) our own agenda, whether it be an ethnocentric or a present-minded perspective or the pursuit for easy pleasure and entertainment.[11]

Because the exclusion of some forms of art appreciation as inappropriate rests on ethical grounds, the analogy with art argument turns out to dissolve into the ethical argument. Thus, we do have a reason to exclude some forms of appreciation of nature as inappropriate, as the proponent of the science-based approach insists, but only on the ground that they fail to take nature on its own terms.

The second claim made by the robust pluralist is that we can take nature on its own terms even when we treat it as, or imagine it to be, something that it is not. That is, showing respect for nature does not necessarily require us to treat it as the sort of thing that it is. This second claim opens the door for admitting, as appropriate, forms of appreciation that were excluded by the science-based approach and also by Moderate Pluralism. Take the aesthetic appreciation of natural things in light of tales from mythology and folklore, for instance. As we have seen, proponents of the latter approaches object to this sort of appreciation on the grounds that it displays a sort of disregard for nature as an autonomous thing. But the robust pluralist disagrees. It is true that some instances of such appreciation do this, but mythological or folktale-based approaches to appreciation need not be problematic in this way; some can be just as appropriate or correct as scientifically informed appreciation, formal appreciation or being moved by nature.

How does the robust pluralist construe the notion of respecting nature, of taking nature on its own terms, such that this can be? One suggestion, which comes from Saito, is that appreciation takes nature on its own terms when it attempts 'to explain or make sense of observable features of specific natural objects'.[12] The appreciation of the stars in light of the stories of Greek mythology, for example, is an appropriate form of appreciation, on this approach, because it treats the night sky as something that is not man-made, and provides a story that explains why it has the features it does. Saito acknowledges that these sorts of myths and folktales make use of anthropomorphic devices – in them, inanimate things are often portrayed as sentient, for example – and they often invoke plotlines and themes that come from human life. In Greek myth, for example, the explanations for why the constellations are the way they are often turn on the struggles of the gods with very human-like feelings of lust, jealousy and love. But in being anthropomorphic, Saito insists, they are no different from the stories that figure in scientifically informed appreciation, which 'must be told in the language comprehensible to us by utilizing concepts, categories, and explanatory models we construct'.[13] As long as stories treat nature as an autonomous thing worthy of some sort of narrative of its own, appreciation that employs those stories takes nature on its own terms, and respects it. Hence, there is nothing inappropriate about using the stories of myth and folklore as a source for the thought component of nature appreciation *per se*.

Thus, for the robust pluralist, the range of ways in which we can appreciate nature includes not only scientifically informed appreciation, formal appreciation and being moved by nature, but also appreciation in which we draw on folklore and mythology, treating nature as something that we know it is not. But one can extend this range even further, beyond the realm of cultural accounts of nature, such as those from folklore and myth, to accounts drawing on more personal associations. These accounts, more so than the cultural ones mentioned above, are dismissed by other approaches as yielding inappropriate appreciation. But, again, the robust pluralist will insist that once we see the basis for determining what counts as respect for nature, we will find that even some of these accounts can produce perfectly appropriate aesthetic appreciation.

As an example of this, consider the case, described by Ronald Hepburn, where we appreciate weather conditions in a natural environment, seeing 'the storms of nature as having affinity with our own internal storms, [and] nature's stillness as intensifying our potentiality for inner calm'.[14] On Saito's line of thought, such thoughts may not be inappropriate ones to employ in our aesthetic appreciation of nature, so long as, in employing them, we attempt 'to explain or make sense of observable features of specific natural objects'. Thus, if our account of a storm's rage in terms of our emotional upheaval provides an explanation for the particular way it is – the lightning coming from our sudden rage, the billowing clouds emerging from our clouded emotions, the buffeting winds driven by the conflicting desires that we feel – this account may be a perfectly appropriate thought component to bring to our appreciation of the storm.

In addition to the one offered by Saito, a somewhat different conception of what it means to respect nature, or take nature on its own terms, is suggested by Hepburn.[15] In discussing the storm example, Hepburn says that it is not inappropriate to 'inwardly appropriate' the forms of nature to our own feelings and inner states, provided they sharpen our perception and relate to 'fundamental features of the lived human state', and provided that we are aware of the fact that we are projecting our feelings onto nature.[16] Based on these remarks, we might say that we show respect for nature when we do not use it merely as a stimulus for easy enjoyment, but employ its complexity and variety to explore and develop our inner lives in a self-conscious way. The person who looks at the storm and imagines a distant rock as a haunted castle is failing to respect nature, according to this criterion: he simply reaches for an unimaginative and meaningless cliché. The person who projects his own feelings onto the natural scene, in the way described above, in contrast, takes it on its own terms in the sense of responding to what nature has to offer as a stimulus for self-reflection. On either conception of what it means to respect nature, Saito's or one suggested by Hepburn, these more personalized thought components can be seen as providing appropriate forms of appreciation of nature.

But neither are they the 'be all and end all' of nature appreciation, however: for the robust pluralist, appreciation can also be based on science, 'pure form', our emotional responses to nature, and cultural accounts such as myth and folklore. And neither should our more personal responses be seen as *more* appropriate than appreciation based on these other sorts of thought component. Rather, each is equally legitimate, allowing us to grasp one part of the overall aesthetic character of nature.

Given this description, Robust Pluralism may seem very robust indeed; in fact, one might wonder just what, if anything at all, distinguishes it from the post-modern view. The fundamental difference is that the robust pluralist insists, unlike the post-modernist, that not 'anything goes' when it comes to choice of thought component. The pluralist will hold that, just as some instances of art appreciation are to be rejected as inappropriate, so are some instances of nature appreciation. Thinking of a set of mountain peaks as a pair of gigantic breasts may be amusing and lend the peaks a certain visual interest, but it hardly seems as serious an effort at aesthetically appreciating the mountains as, say, appreciating them in light of geological fact or ancient native legend. Even on Robust Pluralism, such appreciation lies beyond the pale of the appropriate. But unlike the more rigid approaches of Formalism, the science-based approach, and even Moderate Pluralism, Robust Pluralism leaves us great latitude in selecting a thought component: we are free to choose among various possibilities, all of which are equally legitimate and appropriate as ways of conceptualizing nature, so far as aesthetic appreciation goes.

The attractions of Pluralism, in both its moderate and robust formulations, are obvious. It allows us to admit that scientific knowledge can play a role in the appropriate aesthetic appreciation of nature, without having to assign it a privileged status. It also vindicates the idea that the aesthetic appreciation of nature is an experience characterized, at some fundamental level, by freedom. As mentioned in our discussion of the post-modern view in Chapter 2, the possibility of freely bringing all sorts of ideas and associations to bear in appreciating nature is, for many, one of the chief attractions of nature as an aesthetic object. Pluralism legitimates this freedom, while still allowing us to set some limits upon what we count as appropriate or correct aesthetic appreciation. Finally, Robust Pluralism, perhaps more so than any of the other positions we have considered, allows us to see the aesthetic value of nature as having deep personal significance. That it has such significance, providing a way of better understanding our inner lives, is another strong intuition that many of us have about the aesthetics of nature. In short, Pluralism seems to offer us many of the positive features of the post-modern view, but without its serious drawbacks.

OBJECTIONS TO PLURALISM

The tenability of Pluralism, however, hinges on a particular claim about the two main arguments put forward by the proponent of the science-based approach. For her view to be correct, the pluralist must be right when she says that these arguments, when properly understood, lead to the conclusion that many different sorts of thought content are equally appropriate for aesthetic appreciation. But defenders of the science-based approach argue that this is not, in fact, the case. Let us first examine the claims made by the proponent of Robust Pluralism to the effect that the ethical argument supports her approach, rather than a science-based one.

According to the robust pluralist, we need not conceive of nature in terms of factual accounts of its make-up, composition and behaviour, in order to 'appreciate it on its own terms', or adopt a properly respectful stance towards it. Consider Saito's criterion for respecting nature, for example. On that criterion, we adopt a respectful stance as long as we make nature the focus of an account that explains its observable features, whether that be a scientific account, a myth or even, perhaps, a more personal narrative. By doing so, we treat nature on its own terms. The essence of this view is that acknowledging a natural object as an autonomous thing worthy of our focused attention is sufficient to treat it respectfully.

But even if all of this is true, it is hard to see how this could show that the various sorts of appreciation countenanced by the robust pluralist are all equally appropriate, as she wants to claim. For even if it is true that to make something the subject of a fictional account shows some amount of respect for it, one surely shows that thing *more* respect when one makes it the subject of a *true* account of its origin. To put the point differently, to employ a thought component that truly characterizes a natural object is to *further* acknowledge it as an autonomous thing worthy of our focused attention, and so to show greater respect for it.

For example, consider again the case of aesthetically appreciating the stars. According to the robust pluralist, Penny, who thinks of them in terms of the mythological stories about their creation, is treating them 'on their own terms', or respectfully, since her use of those stories is a tacit acknowledgement that the stars are worth considering and attending to. But if that is the case, surely Sam, who thinks of them in terms of the scientific accounts of their creation, goes further in taking them on their own terms. It seems reasonable to think this because whereas the mythological stories about the creation of the constellations are fictional, the scientific stories about their creation are true (or, at least, the most likely to be true of all the stories about their origin that we currently have). Thus thinking about the stars in light of the latter stories would seem to be a greater acknowledgement of the fact that the stars are autonomous things worthy of our attention, since to do so is to give the stars themselves 'greater attention'.

Much the same point can be made in relation to the slightly different gloss on respecting nature that we extracted from Hepburn's remarks. According to that gloss, we show respect for nature when we do not use it merely as a stimulus for easy enjoyment, but employ its perceptual complexity and variety to explore and develop our inner lives in a self-conscious way. To see the various aspects of a storm as corresponding to our own inner turmoil is to show respect for it, on this conception, whereas to use nature merely as a backdrop for clichéd and unimaginative fantasizing is not. It may be true that to employ nature in a complex exploration of our inner lives is to accord it a modicum of respect: to do so is at least to recognize that nature's appearance is sufficiently interesting for it to be useful for psychological discovery. But even if this is true, to recognize, not merely nature's complexity, but its various other characteristics also, is surely to accord it a greater amount of respect, to take it more fully on its own terms. If this is correct, then it would seem that, contrary to the robust pluralist's analysis of the situation, the ethical argument really does favour one sort of appreciation, namely the scientifically informed variety, over other sorts. Since the robust pluralist views the analogy with art argument as collapsing into the ethical argument, this yields the more general conclusion that the arguments offered in favour of the science-based approach do, in fact, favour one sort of thought component, namely the scientifically informed, over other sorts.

The robust pluralist can object that, for all of this, his doctrine is true: for he has shown, if nothing else, that some instances of appreciation that employ fictitious characterization of the object's origin and character are not *entirely* inappropriate, involving as they do some level of acknowledgement of the worth of nature. Hence, the category of appropriate aesthetic appreciation must include the afore-mentioned forms of appreciation in addition to scientifically informed appreciation, and this is enough to make Robust Pluralism true. But this is a rather hollow victory, preserving the letter but not really the spirit of Pluralism. For even if we say that we have proven aesthetic appreciation pluralistic, the pluralist's own principles (i.e. the ethical argument) entail that it is best, or most appropriately, carried out when using true characterizations of the object's origin and character (e.g. characterizations from natural science). 'Pluralism' is a misleading name for this situation, suggesting as it does the existence of multiple, equally valid alternatives. For in this situation, forms of appreciation that employ fictitious characterizations of the object's origin and character are not equal to scientifically informed appreciation; rather, they are poor cousins.

What about the more moderate version of Pluralism? The moderate pluralist has no desire to show that appreciation that employs fictitious characterizations of nature is appropriate; rather, she aims only to show that appreciation whose thought component is based on 'common sense' characterizations, or merely on perceptual form itself, can be appropriate. Thus, the moderate pluralist is content to claim that formal aesthetic judgements and judgements about our being moved by nature are just as appropriate as scientifically informed ones are. The moderate pluralist claims this because she takes the ethical argument and the analogy with art argument to support all of these forms of aesthetic appreciation equally well. Here also, however, the proponent of the science-based view will argue that, on closer inspection, this is not the case.

With respect to the ethical argument, the case will be analogous to the one described above in discussing Robust Pluralism. In appreciating natural things formally, for instance, by simply attending to their lines, shapes and colours, we take them on their own terms in the sense that we regard their lines, shapes and colours as worthy of our attention. And in appreciating natural things by being moved by them, we take them on their own terms in the sense that we regard their obvious perceptual features – their size, power, and so forth – as worthy of our attention. But even if this is all true, it would still seem true that to appreciate natural things in light of, not only their lines, shapes and colours, and their obvious perceptual features, but also their various other qualities – their origins, say, or their ecological functions – is to accord them greater respect, to take them 'on their own terms' to a greater degree. If this is correct, then it is scientifically informed aesthetic appreciation which is given pride of place, as it were, by the considerations adduced in the ethical argument. Thus the moderate pluralist is mistaken in saying that science-based appreciation does not possess any special or privileged place in the aesthetics of nature, but is merely one of a plurality of equally valid forms of appreciation.

Now this line of argument alone may not sway the moderate pluralist, for unlike the robust pluralist, the moderate pluralist sees the ethical argument as distinct from the analogy with art argument, and he may be inclined to simply disregard the former. He may grant that such explicitly ethical considerations favour scientifically informed appreciation of nature over other forms of appreciation, but respond by saying: 'so much the worse for those ethical considerations'. The proper relation between ethical and aesthetic matters is, after all, complicated and widely debated.[17] Instead, he may insist that we ought to be guided by more clearly aesthetic considerations, such as those that emerge by drawing the analogy with art. And he will insist that this analogy, when properly understood, does allow us to view formal appreciation, scientifically informed appreciation, and being moved by nature as equally appropriate ways in which to regard nature.

The idea here is that, in appreciating art, formal appreciation and 'being moved' can be just as appropriate as appreciation that is more informed by art history and art theory. Consider again the examples pointed to by the moderate pluralist: delighting in the juxtaposition of colours in a fresco by Raphael, without knowing anything about the work's genre, or anything about the art historical developments of which it is a part, and Carroll's example of children being emotionally moved by the capers in *commedia dell'arte*. These kinds of appreciation focus upon different aesthetic qualities than would be apparent to a connoisseur who is well-informed about art history and art theory, but there is no difference in the status of these different kinds of aesthetic qualities. As Carroll puts it in discussing being moved by nature, such appreciation need not 'be regarded as any less deep' than appreciation informed by art history and art theory.[18]

The proponent of the science-based view, however, will question this claim about the aesthetic appreciation of art.[19] In fact, she will suggest that the pluralist's own examples suggest the opposite view. Consider again Carroll's example of being moved by an artwork. The response that he picks out is a child-like response: in fact, it is not only child-like, it is, literally, a child's response. According to Carroll, we ought not to consider such aesthetic appreciation 'any less deep' than the aesthetic appreciation of the art-historically informed theatre connoisseur. But this is, intuitively, somewhat implausible. The child-like response of amusement may not be an inappropriate response to have to a *commedia dell'arte*, and it may, in fact, be the initial aesthetic response that most viewers of the work have. But would anyone regard this child-like response and the judgement of a seasoned and informed theatre critic as equally significant insights into a particular work's aesthetic achievement? Consider another example that Carroll cites: a person who responds emotionally to musical fanfare, finding it stirring.[20] According to Carroll, such a person can 'objectively assert that it is stirring without any knowledge of music history and its categories'. But even if that is the case, it does not seem that the observation that a musical work contains stirring fanfare sheds as much light on that work's aesthetic achievement as, say, a music critic's description of its bold, expressive compositional structure.

What this suggests is that, as in the case of the robust pluralist, what the moderate pluralist has succeeded in extracting from arguments initially offered to support the science-based view is something less than *bona fide* pluralism. The pluralist is correct in claiming that the scope of appropriate aesthetic appreciation includes forms of appreciation apart from the scientifically informed variety: formal appreciation, and being moved by nature. But the special status of the former entails the lack of a genuinely pluralistic range of equally viable options. On this view, then, the upshot of the pluralistic critique is not, ultimately, a displacement of the science-based approach, but rather a clearer conception of what precisely this approach involves.

CHAPTER 6

NATURE AND THE DISEMBODIED AESTHETIC

So far, our discussions of the aesthetics of nature have been premised on a traditional philosophical definition of the concept of aesthetic quality, which we introduced at the end of Chapter 2: an aesthetic quality is a visual or auditory appearance that is pleasing or displeasing *for its own sake*. In the previous chapters, we have examined some different ways in which philosophers have tried to understand the appreciation of aesthetic qualities, so defined, as this occurs, or ought to occur, in nature.

One important – and as we noted, controversial – aspect of this definition is its restriction of the experience of aesthetic qualities to the so-called 'higher' or 'distal' senses of vision and hearing. In this chapter we take up the controversy over this restriction. As we will see, this controversy has a particular salience for the aesthetics of nature, given the special difficulties involved in applying the traditional, more restrictive definition to natural things. In particular, we will examine the claim of Arnold Berleant that closer attention to the aesthetics of nature provides us with a compelling case for abandoning the traditional definition in favour of a quite different understanding of the nature of the aesthetic: the so-called 'aesthetics of engagement'.

THE CHALLENGE TO THE DISEMBODIED AESTHETIC

When we introduced our philosophical definition of 'aesthetic quality' in Chapter 2, we noted that, because it excludes pleasures experienced through the 'lower senses' of smell, touch and taste, it could be described as portraying aesthetic pleasure as 'transcending the body', or 'disembodied'. To better situate the debate over this aspect of our definition in relation to nature aesthetics, it will be useful to draw out a further implication of this notion of disembodiment: the need for physical distance between the aesthetic appreciator and the object of her appreciation.

If aesthetic appreciation of an object, appreciation of its aesthetic qualities, requires us to experience a disembodied pleasure – that is, one not felt directly in any region of the body – then aesthetic appreciation will generally require our seeing or hearing the object. But this, in turn, is best facilitated by the existence of some physical separation between the object and us, for two reasons. First, if the object that we are appreciating comes into physical contact with us, we may simply lose sight of it. Second, even if this does not occur, when the object comes into physical contact with us, it may bring about various embodied pleasures or displeasures that distract us from seeing or hearing the object. Consider, for example, aesthetically appreciating a piece of clothing, such as a jacket or a dress. It seems that, from the point of view of the traditional definition of the aesthetic, such appreciation is optimally carried out when the item is at some physical distance from oneself: on a rack, for example, or worn by another person. When the item comes into direct physical contact with us, as when we are wearing it, for instance, aesthetic appreciation becomes more difficult. First, we can lose sight of the garment as a whole: we may need to rely on a mirror just to get a good look at it. Second, various embodied pleasures or displeasures caused by our contact with the object can distract us from its look. The garment may be uncomfortable, for example, causing us to itch or chafe. None of this makes it impossible to aesthetically appreciate an item with which we are in physical contact, of course. But it does point to difficulties that we can simply avoid altogether by maintaining a little physical distance from the object of appreciation.

The idea of aesthetic appreciation as facilitated by physical separation from the object of appreciation further reinforces the traditional definition's conception of aesthetic appreciation as essentially a calm, contemplative activity, in which we are to avoid getting too close to things, or becoming too physically involved with them. Instead, we stand apart from things, savouring a disembodied pleasure in perceiving their visual and auditory appearances.

When we think about the traditional conception of aesthetic appreciation in this way, however, a clear tension emerges between that conception and some particular features of nature as an object of aesthetic appreciation. In the case of traditional artworks, such as paintings, sculpture and musical works, obtaining the requisite sort of distance is fairly easy. In the gallery, we view paintings from an optimal distance, for example. But when we move into nature, things are often quite different. Unlike a painting, which is content to hang immobile on the gallery wall, the natural environment that you are trying to appreciate may well blast you with icy winds and drench you with rain, or surprise you with a sensation of warmth when the sun suddenly breaks through the clouds on a chilly day. The basic difficulty is that, given its tendency to envelop us and impinge upon us, it is more difficult to maintain physical distance from nature and, therefore, more difficult to attain the contemplative, disembodied pleasure required for aesthetic appreciation.

The proponent of the traditional definition of the aesthetic will respond to this by saying that existence of this tension between the traditional definition and the particular features of nature as an aesthetic object does not mean that there is anything wrong with the traditional definition. Nor does it mean that aesthetic appreciation of nature is impossible. It does mean that aesthetic appreciation is, generally speaking, more difficult in the natural world than it is in the realm of art: as Bell put it, aesthetic experience needs to be 'won from' nature. Unlike artworks, nature does not always cooperate in producing the circumstances conducive to aesthetic appreciation, and we may have to engage in extra work to ensure that those circumstances are in place.[1] But if we make the effort required, aesthetic experience, as conceived by the traditional definition, can be had in the natural world.

There is, however, a very different response to the existence of the afore-mentioned tension between the traditional definition and the particular features of nature as an aesthetic object. In a series of books and essays, Arnold Berleant has argued that the 'lack of fit' between the traditional definition of the aesthetic and the particular features of nature as an aesthetic object does not indicate that there is a problem, or a 'sub-optimality', as we might say, with nature as an aesthetic object. Rather, it indicates a problem with the traditional definition of the aesthetic. Berleant argues for this view by pointing out some cases in which that definition, with its attendant notion of physical distance from the object of appreciation, fails to accurately describe aesthetic appreciation in the arts. To provide the flavour of Berleant's argument, we will consider three specific cases that he discusses: sculpture, theatre and literature.

According to Berleant, the traditional definition of the aesthetic distorts our experience of sculpture in that modern sculpture, to be properly appreciated, must often be touched. 'Appreciating certain sculptures', he writes, 'requires walking into or through them, climbing upon them, or repositioning their parts'.[2] One of Berleant's examples is a sculpture by Mark di Suvero called *Atman* (1985). This work consists of a tepee-like arrangement of large iron beams, hanging from which is a swing on which people are free to sit.[3] Unless you actually touch this work, sitting on it and gazing up at the structure surrounding you, you are missing a vital aspect of the work. Berleant thinks that the traditional definition of the aesthetic distorts our experience of sculpture in a deeper way, however. In most situations, unlike the case of *Atman*, we are explicitly told not to touch sculptural works. Berleant claims, however, that 'sculpture, nominally a visual art, is not primarily visual in appeal but tactile'.[4] When we confront a work of sculpture, even if we do not feel the work with our hands, we must imagine or remember the tactile qualities it has, and this plays a key role in our aesthetic appreciation. As Berleant puts it, 'the tactile urge, undeveloped and unencouraged as it is, reveals itself surreptitiously . . . and becomes a fissure in the rock of aesthetic respectability'.[5]

Berleant raises similar points with respect to theatre. Here he points to experimental forms of theatre involving audience participation as evidence of the need for a different understanding of the aesthetic. He mentions the Open Theatre's 1968 production of Jean-Claude van Itallie's play *The Serpent: A Ceremony*, in which the actors spilled off the stage, offering apples to the audience, all as a part of the play.[6] Since the audience is, literally, a part of the play, it would be impossible for audience members to maintain physical distance from the art work in this case. For if they were to do so, they would largely be missing the point of the play. Berleant draws the same conclusion also from a consideration of modern literature. Although we cannot place literary works in physical locations in the way that we can locate sculptures and performances of plays, here again Berleant finds the idea of distancing ourselves from the work misleading. Literary works such as James Joyce's novel *Ulysses*, he points out, demand that the reader participate, contributing 'to the work's coherence by discerning the order hidden amid the thick flow of events and thoughts'.[7]

In each of these cases, Berleant argues, the appreciator of the artwork would be mistaken to attempt to impose or maintain distance between her and the object she is appreciating. If she were to do so, she would miss important aspects of the work, and perhaps even misjudge it altogether. Berleant takes this to suggest that the traditional definition of the aesthetic as 'disembodied pleasure or displeasure' is flawed: it fails to describe the aesthetic experiences of art that people actually have. For this reason, we ought to reject it in favour of a better definition.

Berleant thinks that his examples also suggest such a definition. In the cases described above, it is clear what the appreciator needs to do, in order to aesthetically appreciate these works correctly, and this is exactly the opposite of what the traditional definition says. She ought to try to diminish or remove the distance between herself and the object, *engaging with* the object that she is trying to appreciate. For example, she ought to walk in, and through, large works of sculpture, and she ought to become an active participant in the events of the play. Correspondingly, she also ought to freely use all her senses, not only vision and hearing, to appreciate the work. Berleant sums up his view this way:

> While the model of separation and distance may serve useful purposes in analysis, scholarship, and criticism, that standard misleads our experience of art by placing it under external constraints. Contemplative theories impede the full force of art and misdirect our understanding of how art and the aesthetic actually function. A theory of engagement, in contrast, responds directly to the activities of art as they occur most distinctively and forcefully.[8]

According to Berleant's approach, the notion of engagement between the appreciator and the object appreciated becomes the central idea in the concept of the aesthetic. For Berleant, this notion of engagement is not simply any old kind of interaction, however. He understands it as a joining of 'perceiver and object into a perceptual unity'.[9] What this means is that the object of appreciation, as a separate and distinct thing, dissolves away, becoming inextricably mingled with the perceiver. What I appreciate is not so much an object, then, as an *experience* that encompasses both me and the object in an inseparable whole. For example, in the theatre case, aesthetic experience is not so much a matter of attending to an independent event that is distinct from us; rather it is a matter of attending to the experience we have while we are engaged in the play. Berleant's engaged aesthetic, then, represents a radical reversal of the traditional definition. Instead of taking us outside of, or transcending, the self, aesthetic experience essentially involves that self, on Berleant's view.

AN ENGAGED AESTHETIC FOR NATURE

The move to a definition of the aesthetic based on engagement, rather than disembodiment, has important implications for the aesthetic appreciation of nature. It means that, as Berleant puts it, the aesthetic appreciation of nature is not 'contemplation but total engagement, a sensory immersion in the natural world that reaches the still-uncommon experience of unity'.[10] Under the more traditional definition, aesthetic appreciation in nature appeared difficult, at least in comparison to the appreciation of art. Natural environments tend to envelop us physically, reducing the physical distance between us and that which we are trying to appreciate. But if we adopt a definition of aesthetic experience in terms of engagement, just the same characteristic will make nature seem an ideal location for aesthetic experience, since nature tends to draw us into a sensory immersion.

In fact, one might think that it is the appreciation of nature, much more than art appreciation, that ought to be considered the paradigm or model for aesthetic experience, on the aesthetics of engagement. For even if Berleant is correct in claiming that many artworks require and invite our participation, few artworks can reduce that distance as quickly and totally as certain natural environments can. Think, for instance, how quickly and forcefully a freezing wind can strike one, or how completely one can be enveloped in a violent rainstorm or within the depths of a dark forest. Or consider the way in which one is enveloped, literally, when one dives into a lake or a pile of autumn leaves.

In picking out these sorts of experiences as paradigms of aesthetic experience, the aesthetics of engagement, echoes, and draws on, the more traditional category of the sublime.[11] As mentioned in Chapter 1, experience of the sublime typically involves an encounter with a natural thing that is in some way overpowering or overwhelming, such as a great waterfall or a high mountain. In these encounters, we can feel as if we are being, or are about to be, 'swallowed up' by some vast object. This same sense of an imminent unity with nature becomes central in the aesthetics of engagement.

The aesthetics of engagement, however, also differs in important respects from the sublime. Philosophers have disagreed about exactly what sublime experience involves, but in general they have taken it to involve something more than this feeling of being 'swallowed up' by a natural object. Edmund Burke, for example, thought that the sublime essentially involves some degree of fear in response to nature. As Burke put it, fear or terror is 'the ruling principle of the sublime'.[12] Other analyses of the sublime highlight a form of self-respect that is produced by our encounter with the vast or overpowering. Immanuel Kant, for instance, claimed that powerful objects in nature 'make our capacity to resist into an insignificant trifle in comparison with their power' and 'allow us to discover within ourselves a capacity for resistance of quite another kind'.[13] On Kant's view, what pleases us in our experience of wild and powerful nature is the fact that it makes plain to us the specific ways in which we are superior to nature: namely, our morality and rationality. On views of sublime experience such as those of Burke and Kant, our sense of being 'swallowed up' by nature is merely one part of a more complex response. The engaged aesthetic, in contrast, places the sense of 'being swallowed up' at the heart of aesthetic experience, and does not characterize the experience primarily in terms of other notions such as fear or self-regard. Therefore, we ought to view the sublime an inspiration for an engaged aesthetic for nature, not as identical to it.

This point, however, raises the question of exactly how we ought to characterize the engaged aesthetic for nature. So far we have heard that it involves a unity of appreciator and natural object, so as to produce an experience that is the focus of our aesthetic scrutiny. What can we add to this description? We can extract some additional qualities from Cheryl Foster's recent characterization of one kind of aesthetic experience of nature. According to Foster, in this kind of experience, 'we encounter nature as an enveloping other, a place where the experience of one's self drifts drastically away from the factual everyday'.[14] Foster calls this sort of experience the 'ambient dimension of the aesthetic value of nature', but the central idea in her account of it is that of engagement or immersion of the self into nature.

Foster's account brings out three important features of the state of being engaged with nature. The first is the prominent involvement of the so-called 'lower' senses: taste, smell and especially touch. As Foster puts it, engagement involves a 'feeling of being surrounded by or infused with an enveloping, engaging tactility'.[15] To be fully engaged with nature, we must do more than simply look and listen: we have to come into more visceral and immediate contact with it. Thus we must feel the wind on our skin, smell the scents that emanate from natural things and touch these things. If we really do mean to reduce the physical distance between nature and us to zero, then this means that the lower senses will come into play as natural objects draw within range of the senses of smell and, ultimately, taste and touch.

The second feature of engagement with nature that emerges from Foster's account is that it involves a diminishment of the role played by thought. As we defined 'thought' in Chapter 2, thinking involves what philosophers call 'propositions': things that can be asserted or denied, and which may be true or false. We can think of propositions, therefore, as describing states of affairs or situations, such as 'the cat is on the mat' or 'two and three equal five'. When we think about nature, we consider situations that involve it, such as 'the crow is in the elm tree', or 'this plain was produced by the recession of a glacier'. As we have seen, some approaches to the aesthetics of nature assign such thoughts an important role. In engaged appreciation, however, the activity of thinking recedes; as Foster says, it remains 'implicit or in the background of consciousness'.[16] This does not mean that, when engaged with nature, we cannot think at all. But it does mean that thinking does not, ultimately, play a central or prominent role in the experience.

Why would one hold that thinking cannot play a central role in a fully engaged experience? One basis for connecting engagement and a diminished role for thinking emerges in Foster's remark that, as thinking recedes, 'the usual habit of cognitive separation into categories dissipates', causing us to experience the world in a 'more diffuse and unified manner'.[17] The idea here is this. In typical, everyday experience, we divide the world into self and non-self. For example, I distinguish the colours of the leaves that hang in the trees around me (non-self) from the hunger in my belly or the itch on my leg (self). This separation of self from non-self seems to be one of the basic features of human psychology. The aim of engagement, however, is to overcome this separation, to weld nature and observer into 'a perceptual unity'. One way to facilitate this is to stop thinking, since if we do so, we will, seemingly, lose our grasp on where (self or non-self) these different sensations come from and reside. What we are left with is no more than a jumble of felt sensations, or what William James called a 'bloomin, buzzin confusion': some colour sensations, an itch, a pang of hunger. If we remove thoughts such as 'this itch sensation resides in me' and 'that colour sensation comes from a leaf that is outside of me', then this jumble of sensations, which is a thorough melding of the object and the observer, is all that remains. Foster gives the example of our experience walking though a forest:

> The textures of earth as we move over them, the sounds of the winds and the wildlife and trees, the moistness or dryness of the air, the nascent colors or seasonal mutations – all can melt into a synthesized backdrop for ambient contemplation of both the backdrop itself and the sensuous way we relate to it.[18]

In this way, then, a diminishment of thinking seems capable of enhancing our degree of engagement with nature, perhaps even necessary for such engagement.

The third feature of the state of engagement with nature that emerges from Foster's description is related to this diminishment of the role of thought. It is the ineffability of this state, its resistance to 'direct or clear expression in discursive prose'.[19] Although she is able to identify some of its main features, including those features just discussed, in her description, Foster maintains that ultimately, the state of engagement cannot be adequately captured by a linguistic description. The idea here is that, since the state of engagement is one of an undifferentiated unity of sensations, any linguistic description of that state will in some way distort its character by introducing the very distinctions among sensations that the state itself erases. For instance, in her description of the experience of walking through a forest, cited above, the engaged state that she is describing is supposed to be a 'synthesis' of various sensations that have all 'melted' together. But her description necessarily pulls them apart from one another: tactile textures are represented as felt in the body, and sounds and colours portrayed as coming from outside. We need these descriptions because without them, we cannot really get a handle on what is involved in the synthesis that Foster is referring to. But we need to remember that such descriptions always misrepresent the final synthesis characteristic of engagement.

CRITICISMS OF THE ENGAGED AESTHETIC

The idea of an aesthetics of engagement for nature can have strong intuitive plausibility, at least when one thinks of applying it to nature. For virtually everyone, at some time or another, has enjoyed an experience of 'sensory immersion' in nature. As children, we delight in plunging into a pile of crisp autumn leaves, and a midnight swim in a mountain lake can be a memorable and invigorating delight. But the question that we need to ask in considering the aesthetics of engagement is not whether engagement with nature, in the sense Berleant describes, is pleasurable or valuable. There is no question that it can be, at least in some cases. The question we need to ask is whether we ought to view engaged experience as the essence of *aesthetic* experience of nature, as Berleant claims we should.

One set of problems arising for the claim that aesthetic appreciation of nature consists in engagement arises from by now familiar ethical considerations pertaining to nature and our relationship to it. In considering other theories of the aesthetic appreciation of nature, such as Formalism

and Post-modernism, we have seen how running afoul of these considerations has made them, in the eyes of some, less satisfactory. How does
the engaged aesthetic fare in relation to these ethical considerations?

One of the considerations at issue is the influence of a particular view
of the aesthetics of nature on the utility of aesthetic considerations in
environmental decision making. According to some, it is a virtue in a
view of the aesthetic appreciation of nature if that view allows aesthetic
value to be used in justifying the preservation of a threatened natural
area. It is difficult, however, to claim this virtue for the engaged aesthetic. In large part this stems from the ineffability of the experience
of engagement. If the aesthetic value of a natural thing or area is to be
offered as a serious reason for preserving it from development or some
other human disturbance, it would seem that this value ought to be communicable to others. Ideally it ought to be as readily communicable as
possible, if it is to be used as a means of swaying the opinion of the relevant decision makers and the general public. But, as we have seen, the
state of engagement is resistant to description, given that it involves a
seamless melting together of sensations with a minimal thought component. As Foster describes it, engagement 'does not rely *in practice* upon
any standards, frameworks, or narratives external to the experiencing
individual'.[20] But without any such standards, frameworks or narratives,
how does one convey the nature, much less the value, of the experience
of engagement to other people? Imagine a defender of a mountain lake
making a case for preserving that area from development in front of a
group of community members, politicians and developers. Without any
way to convey a sense of what aesthetic experience of the area is like, the
preservationist will be hard pressed to convince a sceptical audience of
the value of that experience. 'You just have to experience it for yourself'
is not a particularly useful reply in this context.[21]

It is worth noting that the eschewal in aesthetic experience is something also found in Formalism. Formalists urge us to disregard thoughts
about the natural things that we are appreciating, beyond thoughts
about their visual or auditory form. But when it comes to making
aesthetic value useful in arguments over environmental preservation, the
proponent of an engaged aesthetic is much worse off than the formalist.
For the formalist, the aesthetic value of a natural area consists in
the visual array of lines, shapes and colours that it presents to us. First of
all, these arrays can be described linguistically. The formalist has no
reason to think that saying (truly) that a particular scene contains a
limited range of hues, for example, distorts the nature of the aesthetic

qualities of that scene. On the contrary, such a true description captures those qualities, albeit in a rough and partial way. Second, not only can we describe this array of lines, shapes and colours, we can quantify it using various mathematical techniques: a scenic view can be assessed, for example, in terms of the amount of variation in shape and colour that it offers to the observer. But this sort of quantification of the aesthetic value of a natural area is simply out of the question for the proponent of engaged appreciation. For the sensations that are elements in the engaged experience come from all of the senses, not only vision and hearing. It is unclear whether we could quantify sensations of touch and taste in anything like the way we can quantify visual sensations. And in any case, all of the sensations that figure in the engaged experience are 'melted together' into a seamless unity, rendering any attempt to even number them vain.

Perhaps an even more serious difficulty for the engagement view arises with respect to a different ethical consideration: the notion that appropriate aesthetic appreciation of nature ought to manifest a respectful attitude to nature, or as Saito puts it, take nature 'on its own terms'. According to the aesthetics of engagement, in aesthetically appreciating nature, the idea is for us to merge with nature, producing a sort of unity with it. Nature is treated, in other words, not as a discrete and distinct object that we appraise, but as an element in the production of something else – an experience of unity. One might wonder whether treating nature in this way is to take it on its own terms, or to use it as a mere tool without regard for what it actually is. This suspicion is fuelled by ways that proponents of engagement sometimes talk. In the quotation from Foster cited in the previous section, for instance, note that nature is described as a 'backdrop' for our sensuous experience. She does emphasize that we appreciate the backdrop too (this is inevitable, since all sensations are fused into a unity in the engaged experience), but it remains the backdrop. And in fact it is reasonable to refer to it as the backdrop since on the engaged aesthetic view, all that we do, or can, appreciate of nature is a set of raw sensations produced by our encounter with it. For example, in Foster's example of appreciating a pile of autumn leaves, all one appreciates is the feel of the leaves on your skin, the way they reflect light and the texture of walking on them. Surely to appreciate the leaves 'on their own terms' would be to consider more than simply the kinds of sensations they happen to produce when we fall into a pile of them.

In addition to these worries about the ethical implications of the engaged aesthetic, as applied to nature, philosophers have raised questions about the viability of the engaged aesthetic itself. Recall that the need to adopt an engaged aesthetic rests on the supposed failure of the traditional 'disembodied pleasure' definition to accurately describe the aesthetic appreciation of art. According to Berleant, the engaged aesthetic performs much better here. But is this actually the case? Berleant's paradigm examples of artworks that call for engaged appreciation are contemporary avant-garde artworks, such as experimental theatre and innovative sculptural works. These works do seem to require a departure from the traditional idea of disembodied pleasure, at least in the sense that the observer has to come into physical contact with what he is appreciating. But the defender of the traditional definition of the aesthetic might reply that these works constitute only one portion of the class of artworks as a whole, and that many of the works outside this portion are not well described by an engaged aesthetic. For instance, when we appreciate a fresco by Raphael, we do not contact the work physically. Nor do we participate in the creation of what we appreciate. Or consider an audience member who jumps on stage to join in on the action during a production of *Hamlet*. This person would, no doubt, be more engaged with the play but they would be failing to appreciate the work appropriately, if for no other reason than that their engagement would destroy the action. In other words, the defender of the traditional view might say that, far from an engaged aesthetic providing a better description of the appreciation of art in general, what we ought to say is that both the traditional view and the engaged view describe our appreciation of some, but not all, works of art.

Berleant, as we have seen, would reject this line of thought, arguing instead that the engaged aesthetic is able to cover most, if not all, works of art, including more traditional works, such as a typical production of *Hamlet*. Berleant's argument here is that the appropriate appreciation of these works also requires that we be engaged with them. Thus, for example, Berleant claims that when we read a novel like Joyce's *Ulysses*, we must engage with it to discern 'the order hidden amid the thick flow of events and thoughts'. In the case of traditional theatre, Berleant sees the audience as engaged in virtue of the use of devices such as theatre in the round, where the audience surrounds the stage.[22] But in these examples, the word 'engagement' has come to mean something very different than what it meant when Berleant was discussing his paradigm examples from contemporary avant-garde art. Instead of referring to a physical involvement with the work that results in some sort of experiential unification with the art work, 'X is engaged with the work' now simply means something like 'X is paying close attention to the work'.[23] Berleant is no doubt right that even traditional artworks require engagement, in this sense. In reading a novel like *Ulysses*, we of course are required to pay close attention to the work to discern its theme, plot, and so forth. And in the theatre, if one is seated in closer proximity to the stage, one can pay closer attention to what happens on it. Indeed, it would be hard to find any artwork whose appreciation does not require, or at least would not benefit from, close attention. But this is a different, and much weaker, sense of 'engagement' than that which Berleant employs when describing the engaged aesthetic. Therefore, the fact that these more traditional artworks can be said to be engaged in this weaker sense is just irrelevant to an assessment of Berleant's theory. And since these artworks do not involve engagement in the stronger sense that *does* figure in Berleant's theory, his theory cannot be said to cover any more than one part of the class of artworks.

If it is true that the engaged aesthetic really describes only the appreciation of one sort of artwork, rather than all artworks, we ought to think twice about throwing out the traditional definition of the aesthetic, as Berleant recommends. An alternative response to the cases that Berleant cites would be to say, not that our conception of aesthetic experience is wrong, but that not all art appreciation is aesthetic appreciation. The concepts of art and the aesthetic have been closely associated in Western thought since at least the eighteenth century, and for many people the terms 'artistic' and 'aesthetic' are virtually synonymous. But we need not adopt this practice. In fact, it seems sensible not to, since art can do much besides providing aesthetic pleasure: it can promote a political view, for instance. If we follow this course, then the proper way to interpret Berleant's examples is as showing the extent to which some artists have become interested in facilitating forms of experience other than aesthetic experience, such as engagement.

In fact, there is a very strong reason for drawing *this* conclusion from Berleant's examples, rather than his own conclusion that we ought to discard the traditional definition of the aesthetic for an aesthetics of engagement. This is that the notion of engagement seems incapable of serving as a basis for a definition of the aesthetic. The essential meaning of engagement is the achievement of a sense of unity with an object, through a multisensory immersion in that object. But this kind of experience seems neither necessary nor sufficient for an experience to be aesthetic. It seems unnecessary because we can have experiences that we would call aesthetic without achieving this sense of unity. When we admire the beauty in the face of a passing stranger, or the taut lyricism of some line in *Hamlet*, no feeling of unity, in this specific sense, need be involved. And neither is experiencing this sense of unity sufficient for an experience to be aesthetic. Sexual intercourse is an experience that often involves the experience of a sense of unity with an 'object' (i.e. another person, or at least the body of another person), through a multisensory immersion in that object. But no one, aside from proponents of the engaged aesthetic and related views, would call sexual intercourse an aesthetic experience.[24] If achieving the specific sense of unity constitutive of engagement is neither necessary nor sufficient for an experience to be aesthetic, then we must conclude that engagement does not, after all, reveal anything about the nature of the aesthetic.[25]

This may seem to leave us back where we started, with the traditional definition of the aesthetic as generally restricted to sight and hearing, and the consequent fact that aesthetic experience in nature, though possible, is not always very easily carried off. Perhaps a portion of the motivation for considering an aesthetics of engagement stems from a basic dissatisfaction with this situation. To say that nature is not optimal as an object of aesthetic appreciation might seem to somehow diminish the stature, or worth, of nature as such an object. However, one could also look at this situation in a more positive light. First, the fact that nature is less conducive to aesthetic experience than art ought not to surprise anyone, since nature, unlike at least some art, was not arranged for the purposes of providing such experience. Second, we might think of nature's resistance to aesthetic experience not as an obstacle that breaks up and diminishes this experience, but rather as a challenge that increases its complexity and richness. The fact that aesthetic experience must sometimes be 'won from' nature could be seen as making that experience more, rather than less, valuable and worth having.

CHAPTER 7

AESTHETICS AND THE PRESERVATION OF NATURE

One important goal of the environmental movement in general is to save natural things and areas from degradation or destruction. This aim is motivated by an appreciation of the extent to which human activities have led to species extinction and other sorts of ecological harm. This general aim, however, can be interpreted in two different ways.

One approach is that taken by conservation groups that work for the continued existence and health of natural organisms and ecosystems. Conservationists pursue this work because they believe that the natural organisms or areas in question provide some practical benefit for humanity. They aim to protect these organisms or areas in order to ensure that future generations of humans will be able to reap these benefits by exploiting them. Thus, a conservation organization like Ducks Unlimited Canada works to maintain healthy wetlands and waterfowl populations, but does not oppose the hunting of those waterfowl. On the contrary, it is partly to ensure that such uses of natural resources can continue that Ducks Unlimited does what it does.

Nature conservation, then, understands the goal of saving natural things as, ultimately, a form of prudence in managing limited and fragile resources for human use. However, some environmentalists understand this goal quite differently, as one of preserving, rather than conserving, nature.[1] The preservation of nature involves saving natural things or areas from degradation or destruction, not so that they can be exploited by future generations, but simply so that they can continue to exist as they are. Preservation, unlike conservation, thus does not rest upon any practical benefit that nature has for humanity. Thus, to pursue nature preservation is to assume that nature has value beyond the practical benefits that it can provide for us.

But what, then, is this non-practical value that serves as the basis for preserving nature? One attractive candidate is nature's aesthetic value; in this chapter, we explore the pros and cons of casting aesthetic value in this role.

AESTHETIC PRESERVATION IN THEORY AND PRACTICE

As we noted in Chapter 2, the idea of preserving nature in virtue of its aesthetic value is sometimes called 'Aesthetic Preservation'. A number of philosophers have defended some version of this position. Aldo Leopold explicitly included aesthetic considerations in his influential 'Land Ethic', claiming that 'a thing is right when it tends to preserve the integrity, stability, and beauty of the biotic community'.[2] More recently, other philosophers have also argued that aesthetic value ought to be one consideration that we take into account in deciding how to act with respect to nature. Holmes Rolston argues that environmental ethics needs some concept of aesthetic value in order to be 'adequately founded'.[3] Allen Carlson defends Aesthetic Preservation more explicitly in advocating a version of what he calls 'the eyesore argument': certain forms of human intrusion into nature make it aesthetically worse; therefore we ought not to engage in these forms of intrusion.[4] And other philosophers have defended even stronger versions of Aesthetic Preservationism. Eugene Hargrove's book *The Foundations of Environmental Ethics* (1989) gives pride of place to the aesthetic value of nature: according to Hargrove, the aesthetic value of nature provides the best motivation we currently have for preserving it. Eliot Sober, after considering various other reasons for attempting to preserve nature, settles on its aesthetic value as the most defensible.[5]

Aesthetic Preservation is not merely an invention of philosophers, however. Many actual debates about environmental preservation involve aesthetic considerations. Real life debates about natural preservation are often complex, of course, and many factors besides aesthetic value come into play here. But aesthetic value does play a role: indeed, in the minds of many, aesthetic value is the factor that springs most readily to mind when a cherished natural area is threatened with damage or destruction. As Rolston puts it, 'Ask people, "Why save the Grand Canyon or the Grand Tetons" and the ready answer will be, "Because they are beautiful. So grand!"'[6] To focus our discussion, it will be useful to briefly review a few real life examples of Aesthetic Preservation.

One example of aesthetic considerations in action is the case of the Harris island superquarry in Scotland.[7] This proposed development would have involved digging an enormous pit for mineral extraction on the remote island of Harris in the Hebrides. The pit was supposed to be 1 km by 2 km in area, and extend some 180 m below sea level. Emily Brady describes the potential aesthetic impact of the quarry as 'a great white gouge out of the landscape, as if someone had literally wounded the landscape'.[8] Although opponents of the quarry cited a number of objections to the proposal, the aesthetic impact was, in their view, an important one. They used dramatic before and after photographs to highlight the severe changes that the development would cause in the look of the region. Eventually, after several years of legal battles, the company behind the proposal abandoned the project.

A second interesting example is the case of Yew Tree Tarn, a small lake in the English Lake District.[9] This particular lake happens to be draining due to the opening of an underground fault. The National Trust, a charitable organization that protects important natural areas in the United Kingdom, intervened in order to prevent this draining from occurring. The Trust described its actions as aiming to preserve the beauty of the lake and the surrounding area; in their words, 'the area has been landscaped to ensure its beauty is permanent'.[10]

A third example, more familiar to North American readers, is the contentious proposal to drill for oil in the Arctic National Wildlife Refuge.[11] This area on the northeast coast of Alaska, bordering the Yukon, was designated a protected area by the United States government in 1960. Today the refuge spans over 7 million hectares, and is home to many animal and bird species, including the large migratory Porcupine Caribou herd, which uses a part of the refuge as its calving grounds. The refuge is almost completely free of human inhabitants, although the Gwich'in people live in proximity to the refuge and have traditionally relied on the Porcupine herd for food and clothing. The refuge also contains significant oil deposits, which has led to proposals to open it to petroleum development. Opponents of these proposals have appealed to various considerations, including potential harm to the Porcupine Caribou herd and, thereby, to the Gwich'in who depend upon it. But the feature that is most prominent in their defences of the refuge is its aesthetic value, or, as one advocacy group's website puts it, its 'unique beauty'.

These three examples show that aesthetic value is an appealing, and sometimes effective, way of convincing the public to endorse nature preservation. But can one really make a *rationally* compelling case for nature preservation on aesthetic grounds? Because it is tangible in the sense of being visible, changes in aesthetic value can have a strong rhetorical impact. Before and after photographs, for instance, have an immediate impact that isn't generated by charts and tables detailing long-term ecological effects. But is there substance beneath this impact? Is maintaining the aesthetic value that we find in nature really a logical basis for preserving it from a proposed development with practical human benefits, such as employment, profit and greater convenience? Or is it simply an effective way of 'pushing people's buttons', thereby mobilizing them to support a preservationist agenda?

Constructing a rationally compelling case for Aesthetic Preservation is trickier than it seems. For starters, the strength of the case for Aesthetic Preservation rests on a number of arguable assumptions, some of which we have already encountered in earlier chapters. One is the assumption that, at least in some instances, certain aesthetic assessments of nature are, at least to some degree, more correct, or appropriate, than others. If this is not the case, aesthetic value will not be a very effective tool in convincing others that nature must be spared, despite the practical benefits that exploiting it could bring. For those that favour the exploitation of natural resources can simply assert that, on their way of regarding nature, it has little aesthetic value. In order to serve as a reason for preserving nature, aesthetic value cannot be merely a matter of 'anything goes'. We need to be able to appeal to some sense in which certain judgements of aesthetic value are more correct or more appropriate than others. What this means is that Aesthetic Preservation entails rejecting the postmodern approach to aesthetically appreciating nature. For, as argued in Chapter 2, that approach renders us unable to say whether any particular natural object or area is 'really' aesthetically good or bad, since there is nothing to choose between thought components that render it aesthetically good and those that render it aesthetically poor.

This may not be a fatal difficulty for Aesthetic Preservation, since, as we have seen, there are other approaches to the aesthetics of nature besides the post-modern view, and some of these (Formalism, for example, and also the science-based approach) do allow us to say that, at least in some instances, certain aesthetic assessments of nature are more correct, or appropriate, than others. But Aesthetic Preservation also requires a second assumption: Positive Aesthetics for nature. Positive Aesthetics is the view that all natural things or areas have at least some significant amount of aesthetic value.[12] This view, or something like it, is an assumption of Aesthetic Preservation because in order for us to argue that a species or area ought to be spared because of its aesthetic value, it has to have some aesthetic value. If the area we are trying to protect turns out to be ugly or aesthetically worthless, we will need to appeal to other considerations to justify its protection. This assumption is particularly pressing for Aesthetic Preservation because many of the areas that need to be preserved from development are precisely those thought to be unattractive:

wetlands, for example, or areas thought to be devoid of 'visual interest'. In defending oil development in the Arctic National Wildlife Refuge, for example, Alaskan Senator Ted Stevens asserted that it is aesthetically worthless:

> I defy anyone to say that that is a beautiful place that has to be pre-served for the future. It is a barren wasteland, frozen wasteland and no caribou there during that period of time at all. The porcupine caribou herd uses the coastal plain for only six to eight weeks. . . . This is what it looks like in the summertime. With one well drilled, there's a six-foot pipe sticking up, the rest of it is just constant, constant, constant tundra, no trees, no beauty at all.[13]

Thus, even if the proponent of Aesthetic Preservation does not accept that *everything* in nature is aesthetically good, she will need to claim that a good deal, it not most, of nature is aesthetically good, if Aesthetic Preservation is to be a widely applicable strategy.

Beyond the idea that some aesthetic appreciation is more correct or appropriate, and the notion of Positive Aesthetics, a third, perhaps less obvious, assumption is also required for Aesthetic Preservation. This is the assumption that when we value an object that is aesthetically good, we value it intrinsically. The concept of intrinsic value is usually explained by drawing a contrast with the more familiar concept of instrumental value. When we value something instrumentally, we do not value it for itself, but only as a means to some end that it allows us to achieve. The value of physical monetary currency (dollar bills, for instance) is a para-digm of instrumental value: we value a hundred dollar bill not for itself, but because of what we can use it to obtain (food, a new shirt, a bottle of scotch). It is the food, the shirt or the scotch that we value, not the piece of paper with a politician's face on it. This is reflected in our lack of concern over the replacement of monetary currency by new forms, when we travel to foreign nations, for example, and even the elimination of it altogether, as occurs in electronic financial exchanges. The loss of a 100-dollar bill is of no concern, in these situations, because we can still achieve the ends that it used to facilitate by using something else. Its value to us was only ever instrumental.[14] When something has intrinsic value, however, we value it for itself, not merely for the ends that it allows us to obtain. When we value something intrinsically, we are not content to lose it, even when something else allows us to achieve the same ends that it did.

The notion of intrinsic value is important for the idea of Aesthetic Preservation because unless the value that we find in nature when we appreciate it aesthetically is intrinsic, nature's aesthetic value will not provide us with a ground for preserving *nature itself.* For example, one might think that the value we take in nature when we aesthetically appreciate it is merely instrumental, because what we really value is the experience of various shapes, colours and sounds, and the aesthetic qualities that we find in these. The actual physical objects that allow us to have these experiences – that is, nature – are only a means to an end, and so not intrinsically valuable. For example, you might think that when one sees a black bear crashing through the forest, what one values in the experience is the set of visual and auditory sensations that this produces: the sight and sound of a large black form noisily ploughing through the underbrush. We don't really care about the bear *per se*; we care about it only because it affords us this unique sensory experience. On this view, the value of nature that emerges from our aesthetic experiences of it is rather like the value of money that emerges from our commercial activity: purely instrumental.

This attitude towards nature has surfaced in some of our previous discussions, particularly in connection with Formalism.[15] But for anyone advocating Aesthetic Preservation, it is a dangerous position to take. For if what we value aesthetically is the aesthetic experience generated by nature, and not nature itself, then any argument based on aesthetic value will only be effective as an argument for preserving the experience, not for preserving nature. When some other means for producing that experience is found, there will no longer be any reason to preserve nature itself. The philosophers Routley and Routley give the example of an imaginary 'wilderness experience machine' that produces precisely the same sensory experience as an actual trip to a wilderness: the same sights and smells, the same feeling of the wind on one's skin, and so on.[16] Were such a machine to be invented, Aesthetic Preservation would no longer give us any reason to preserve nature. Of course, no such machine is currently known to exist, so even if it could not be shown that we value nature intrinsically, Aesthetic Preservation would still give us a reason to preserve actual natural things for the time being. But the idea of producing the experience of nature without nature may not be as far-fetched as it sounds: the development of virtual reality simulators, for example, has scarcely begun. Showing that we value nature intrinsically would make Aesthetic Preservation a more solid basis for the preservation of nature.[17]

Making the case for Aesthetic Preservation, then, is more difficult than it might at first appear. Why then is the idea of basing preservation on aesthetic value so attractive? We have already discussed its rhetorical effectiveness in actual preservation debates. But why do philosophers, who typically insist upon reasoned arguments, rather than rhetoric, also support it? Why not base nature preservation on some other non-practical value instead? One answer to this question is that aesthetic value is, as it were, the only game in town: there simply are not other sorts of non-practical value on which we could ground nature preservation. The idea here is that, despite much effort, philosophers have simply failed to spell out the right sort of value.

The most obvious way of spelling out a kind of value that is possessed by nature but which does not arise from its serving our own practical interests is by turning to the practical interests of other living organisms. We might argue, for instance, that a creature such as a bear has certain needs and interests (food, water, space), just as humans do. And we might contend that, just as we take human interests into account when deciding what is valuable and worth preserving, we ought also to take into account the interests of non-human organisms such as bears. After all, such organisms can suffer and be harmed, in some sense, when these interests are frustrated, as human beings can. This line of reasoning provides us with a clear sense in which natural things have value, albeit one that does not emerge from our own practical interests. Accordingly, it can provide a basis for attempting to preserve some natural things: namely living organisms themselves and those elements of their habitats that directly serve their interests.

However, this line of reasoning will take us only so far in justifying the preservation of nature, because many of the natural things that environmentalists wish to preserve are not of this kind. The examples of actual campaigns for Aesthetic Preservation mentioned above, for instance, are all attempts to preserve inanimate natural things – an island, a lake and a stretch of tundra – that do not have clear interests and needs, in the way that bears do. Of course, these natural areas are home to various creatures whose interests may be thwarted by their destruction. But those who oppose development in the Arctic National Wildlife Refuge, for example, would surely not be mollified if the oil companies agreed to move the entire porcupine caribou herd to some safe location, and *then* drill for oil, nor even if it could be shown that building roads, erecting oil platforms and drilling would not substantially harm the flora and fauna in the reserve at all. It is *the place* itself, in addition to the well-being of the creatures it shelters, that they see as valuable and that, accordingly, they wish to see preserved. But an argument for this course of action cannot be mounted simply by extending the familiar concept of interests, which hangs awkwardly on inanimate objects.

Many philosophers have attempted the difficult task of spelling out some further sort of value in nature that could fill this gap.[18] But we need not judge their efforts here to note that, so far as Aesthetic Preservation goes, all of their toil could be avoided by an appeal to aesthetic value.[19] On the one hand, the idea that natural things, such as lakes or islands, are aesthetically appealing does not commit us to implausible claims about their having interests and needs of their own. There is nothing mystifying or obscure about the idea that inanimate objects can be aesthetically valuable: after all, artworks are (typically) inanimate objects. There is no mystery or obscurity here because the aesthetic value that inanimate objects have comes ultimately from the responses that they cause in human beings. On the other hand, although it is in this sense a 'human value', the aesthetic value of natural things does not reduce to the practical or economic benefits that they bring us. Their value does not arise from our manipulating or using them in any way, but only from our looking and listening to them. Aesthetic value, then, seems to be just what the preservationist wants: it is a reason to preserve nature even though we gain no practical benefit from doing so, and it is also familiar enough to seem intelligible.

TWO ISSUES FOR AESTHETIC PRESERVATION

In our discussion so far, we have been understanding Aesthetic Preservation as the saving of aesthetically valuable natural things or areas from degradation or destruction, not so that they can be exploited by future generations, but simply so that they can continue to exist as they are (i.e. with the aesthetic value they have). But this description of Aesthetic Preservation contains an important ambiguity, since it fails to specify precisely what sort of degradation or destruction it is that is being resisted. On one reading, Aesthetic Preservation would justify us in saving natural things from any and all forms of destruction or degradation, from any source whatever. Thus, Aesthetic Preservation would provide as much basis for us to save a mountain from destruction by a (natural) earthquake, or a forest from being destroyed by a volcanic eruption, as it would for us to save the same mountain from damage due to strip mining, or the same forest from destruction by logging. Let us call this sort of preservation *Strong Aesthetic Preservation*. On a different reading, Aesthetic Preservation would require us to save natural things only when they are threatened by human actions. So on this interpretation, Aesthetic Preservation would not give us a reason to attempt to save a mountain from destruction by an earthquake, but it would give us a reason to attempt to save it from strip mining. We can call this sort of preservationism *Weak Aesthetic Preservation*.

At first glance, Strong Aesthetic Preservation may seem like a silly idea, and a view that no sensible environmentalist would actually endorse. The idea of trying to somehow shield a forest from a volcanic eruption, for instance, seems ludicrous. However, much of the destruction and degradation that nature wreaks upon itself is far smaller in scale than a volcanic eruption, and in these cases, the idea of 'saving nature from itself' can seem more feasible. In fact, one of our examples of an *actual* instance of Aesthetic Preservation, the preservation of Yew Tree Tarn, is just such a case. The drainage of the tarn is entirely due to natural processes that opened an underground fault. Presumably, similar processes have been operating in nature since time immemorial, draining bodies of water just like this one, in just this way. In intervening to preserve the tarn in its current state, the National Trust is not protecting its current aesthetic value from the hand of man, but from the processes of nature itself. Similar cases are not hard to imagine: think of a rare bird species, on the verge of extinction due to some natural cycle of disease or a natural decline in its food supply. If the species was a particularly distinctive one aesthetically, one might argue that we ought to intervene to protect it, by providing food for it, perhaps, or inoculating it against potentially fatal diseases.[20]

In fact, Strong Aesthetic Preservation might seem like the more logical of our two positions, if we reflect on the fundamental idea behind Aesthetic Preservation. That fundamental idea is that we preserve the aesthetic treasures of nature so that others can enjoy them. But if that is the aim, then why should it matter from whence threats to these aesthetic treasures arise? Consider an analogy: imagine that an aesthetically valuable artefact, a great work of art, for instance, or a Lamborghini sports car, is entrusted to your care. If a threat to it arose from a human source – a vandal who wanted to spray paint on it or take a sledgehammer to it, for instance – you would surely see it as your duty to try to protect it, given that it has been entrusted to your care. If the threat arose from a natural source – a hailstorm, or an earthquake say – why wouldn't you do the same? A threat is a threat, after all, and if the fundamental idea is to preserve what is aesthetically valuable, then it seems one ought to attempt to stop any of them that it is possible to stop.

Strong Aesthetic Preservation, however, faces an important objection, which is that it is self-defeating as a way of preserving nature. The idea here is that in preserving a natural thing or area in this way, we make certain of its aspects artefactual. In the example mentioned above of preserving a great art work, or a Lamborghini, it is reasonable to try to protect against damage from things such as hailstorms and earthquakes. This is reasonable because natural forces such as hail are alien to the sort of thing we are trying to protect, which is an artefact. But acting in the same way with respect to things such as lakes is not reasonable in the same way, because hailstorms and geological processes are not alien to natural things such as lakes. On the contrary, lakes are created, and destroyed, by various geological processes. In the case of Yew Tree Tarn, blocking the natural geological processes that are destroying the lake turns it into something that has come about through the voluntary and intentional agency of human beings – that is, an artefact. Consequently, Strong Aesthetic Preservation cannot deliver what the preservationist ultimately wants: the preservation not just of things that currently happen to be natural, but the preservation of those things *as natural*.[21]

The upshot of this objection, then, is that only the weak version of Aesthetic Preservation is coherent as a form of *nature* preservation. The proponent of the Strong version of the view can concede this, but object that only Strong Aesthetic Preservation can be polemically useful in arguing for preservation. The thinking here is this. The preservationist's basic situation is that she wishes to preserve certain natural areas, but discovers that others see them as valueless and so not worth keeping. Before they will support keeping them, these people first want to know what is so valuable about these areas. To convince these people, the preservationist points out the aesthetic value of these areas. If all goes well, this convinces the doubters, who enthusiastically endorse preserving the areas in question on this basis. When these areas are protected from destruction due to natural forces, however, the preservationist objects: we ought not to do *that*, she insists. When asked why, she answers: 'Because then they will no longer be natural areas'. But this will do nothing to sway the people that the preservationist originally converted: their starting point was an inability to see any value in nature *per se*. They simply do not care how much or how little nature there is: this was the entire reason that the preservationist needed to appeal to aesthetic value in the first place. If this line of thought is correct, the account of the fit between nature preservation and aesthetic value sketched in the last section may be overly optimistic: in some cases, at least, aesthetic value may not pull in the direction the preservationist wants it to go.

However the aesthetic preservationist resolves the issue of the strong and weak versions of her doctrine, there is a further set of problems that she also needs to address. The problems in question involve the relative strength of the aesthetic value of nature in relation to practical considerations that weigh against it in debates over preservation. Typically, discussion of this issue shapes up as follows. On the one hand, we have the practical advantages that exploiting a natural area or species will bring: more abundant resources for industry, jobs, more convenient travel, cheaper accommodations, cheaper food or goods for consumers, profit for producers, and so on. On the other hand we have the aesthetic value that is lost through this exploitation. In order for Aesthetic Preservation to be a generally successful strategy, aesthetic value has to outweigh these practical benefits, at least in some reasonable percentage of cases. But is this the case?

Here we confront the difficult task of ranking quite different kinds of value.[22] One extreme view is that aesthetic value is always, or almost always, outranked by other forms of value, including the practical benefits typically associated with environmental development. The justification for this view is that aesthetic merit is a superficial kind of value. In developing this sort of case, J. Robert Loftis draws an analogy between our treatment of nature and our treatment of other persons. Loftis imagines a doctor with only one donor heart but two patients who need a heart transplant. In such a case, he points out, the doctor should appeal only to medical facts in making her decision. If she were to give the heart to one patient because that person was more physically attractive or handsome than the other, she would be making a serious moral error. Further, the ground of that error would be clear: treating what is essentially a superficial and unimportant form of value – aesthetic value – as outweighing other considerations. Based on this sort of analogy, Loftis concludes that 'aesthetic considerations involving nature are weak and cannot motivate the kind of substantial measures environmentalists routinely recommend'.[23] 'How', he asks, 'can environmentalists ask thousands of loggers to give up their jobs and way of life on the basis of aesthetics?'[24]

This particular analogy, however, is a misleading one. It is surely correct to say that the aesthetic value of potential heart transplant recipients does not, and ought not, outweigh medical considerations. But this is an extreme case, where the implications of favouring aesthetic value are as strong as they could possibly be: they are literally a matter of life and death. But typical cases of environmental preservation are not like that: choosing aesthetic value over other considerations does not typically place lives at risk. Choosing aesthetic value always has consequences, of course, and some of these are important: it may reduce income for some, or result in others having to move to find new employment, for example. We might accept that considerations of basic human viability always come first, and trump aesthetic value, but still argue that, in some cases, preserving aesthetic value is worth the cost.[25] The question for such a view is: in these cases, can we say that the aesthetic value of a natural area justifies the cost of preserving it?

One reason for thinking that it might be is that in other areas of life, we do make practical sacrifices for aesthetic value. We spend both private and public money on artworks, for example. These measures have costs: they reduce the income that citizens would otherwise keep for themselves or spend on other things. This seems to show that aesthetic value is not so superficial that *any* other consideration trumps it: sometimes we do sacrifice other valuable things to attain it. In his discussion, Loftis acknowledges this point but objects that the costs of preserving natural beauty far outweigh the costs of funding art. He estimates the economic costs of forgoing development in the Arctic National Wildlife Refuge, for example, at $800 million. This figure, he points out, is much greater than the annual budget of the National Endowment for the Arts, which is around $100 million. Thus, Loftis would have us conclude that Aesthetic Preservation of the environment is simply too expensive. But the financial comparison drawn here is apt to be misleading, in two ways. First, although the economic benefit of exploiting the Arctic National Wildlife Refuge may be substantial, at least according to Loftis' estimate, this may not be the case in other instances. In some instances, developing a mountain into a ski resort, for example, exploiting nature may produce smaller benefits. Second, it is not clear that, even when the costs of environmental preservation are relatively substantial, as in the case of Arctic National Wildlife Refuge, they are too high. Loftis chooses the annual budget of the National Endowment for the Arts as an indication of the upper limit of sacrifice for aesthetic value, but this number seriously underrepresents the sacrifice made for aesthetic value. For one thing, the National Endowment's budget represents only a part of the total amount spent annually on art, which also includes other public and private funds. We also need to consider here other spending on aesthetic value: consider, for instance, the beautification programs run by virtually every sizable town and city, consisting of the maintenance of local gardens, and architectural repair and restoration. And then there is spending on various other aesthetically valuable items: furniture, clothes, houses, cars, and so forth.

On balance, it seems that the view that aesthetic value is so weak that it is *never* capable of outweighing the pragmatic benefits of development is too extreme. How often it actually succeeds in doing so, however, is something that we must assess by examining particular cases.

THE PRESERVATIONIST'S DILEMMA

So far we have documented a number of assumptions necessary to produce a viable argument for Aesthetic Preservation. In this section, we consider one more. In the previous section, we saw that such an argument requires that the aesthetic value that we gain in saving nature from development must outweigh the practical benefits that would accrue to us from that development. But we also need to factor in the aesthetic value of the developed site itself. Aesthetic Preservation requires that there be *a gain* in aesthetic value in saving nature, rather than developing it. In other words, it is a fundamental assumption of Aesthetic Preservation that nature left untouched is *more* aesthetically valuable than the development that would replace it.

This assumption is open to question in two ways. First, one could question it by pointing out that some human developments are aesthetically outstanding. The city of Venice, for instance, is widely considered to be aesthetically excellent. It was built on a marshy lagoon. Even if this lagoon in its natural state was aesthetically outstanding, it seems unlikely that preserving it by forgoing the construction of Venice would have been an aesthetic gain, given the splendour of that city. Even if the widespread view that Venice is aesthetically outstanding is mistaken, such that its construction was an aesthetic loss, it does seem at least possible that in some cases, developing nature could be an aesthetic gain.[26] If this is true, then the assumption that nature left untouched is *more* aesthetically valuable than the development that would replace it is false in general.

Of course, this first objection to the assumption might not be seen as very serious, given that much of the human development currently chewing up natural areas will hardly bear a comparison with Venice. On the contrary, much of it is vulgar, programmatic and uninspired: urban sprawl, strip mines, industrial farms, massive dam projects, and the like. It would seem that in these cases, at least, development is no aesthetic gain. And whatever we might want to say about Venice, these are really the important cases for the aesthetic preservationist, constituting the primary forms of human encroachment into nature. As long as the assumption holds true here, Aesthetic Preservation will remain an effective strategy.

But the assumption can be questioned here also, in a much more fundamental way. One might argue that strip mines, urban sprawl, factory farms and massive dams are actually as aesthetically good as, or better than, the nature they replace. Proponents of one major dam project, for example, defended the development by saying that it would create 'one of the world's great scenic wonders'.[27] At first glance, this may seem to be a cynical ploy by developers to advance their interests, rather than an honest aesthetic judgement. However, there might be a sound basis for the claim that strip mines, urban sprawl, and so on, are aesthetically good. One such basis is 'camp sensibility': a playful attitude that transforms mundane and aesthetically poor items into objects of aesthetic enjoyment.[28] The lesson of camp is that even items that are vulgar, programmatic and uninspired can, when viewed with a sense of irony and playfulness, have a kind of aesthetic value. A camp sensibility takes delight in ridiculous and trashy art: in the gaudy sentimentality of show tunes, for example, or the goofy preciousness of garden gnomes. This attitude can undermine the assumption that nature left untouched is more beautiful than the development that would replace it. Consider urban sprawl, for instance. A camp sensibility might allow us to delight in its meaningless repetition, and revel in its incongruous mishmash of architectural elements. The creation of urban sprawl, in other words, need not be an aesthetic loss to us, as long as we adopt the right sort of attitude to it.

The view can be further developed by stressing some other ways in which human developments, although seemingly devoid of any aesthetic interest on a first glance, may offer us aesthetic pleasure. To a first glance, a strip mine might appear aesthetically poor in virtue of being a huge gash in the earth, emitting a terrible din and spewing black smoke into the sky. But if we consider it not simply as a gash in the earth, but as a large industrial mechanism, it might look quite different. The billowing smoke, loud noise and roaring fires, rather than obtrusive and marring, may seem indicative of its power and vitality. After all, many machines look aesthetically appealing. Further, even if one finds the smoke, noise and fire to be obtrusive and jarring in relation to the landscape, one might even find aesthetic value in this very incongruity. As Yuriko Saito points out, a similar incongruity is often aesthetically appreciated in art, particularly in contemporary works that employ dissonance between elements of the artwork as an artistic technique.[29] And finally, such developments can often be viewed as expressive of certain positive values: hard work, determination and vision, for instance. If we see them in any of these ways, strip mines and their ilk might not look so bad after all.[30]

This sort of conclusion represents a threat to any argument in favour of Aesthetic Preservation, and the proponent of Aesthetic Preservation will want to rebut it. She will want to respond that even if these considerations show that human developments like urban sprawl, strip mines and industrial farms have some aesthetic value, this value will, generally speaking, be much less than the aesthetic value possessed by the natural areas that they replace. But the preservationist must tread carefully here: this supposed difference in value must rest on *purely aesthetic grounds*. Remember again that Aesthetic Preservation is meant to sway those who can see no value in nature that does not serve our practical ends, and thus, no reason to preserve it. But if it turns out that the preservationist's preference for aesthetically appreciating nature, as opposed to urban sprawl, is ultimately based, not on any difference in their aesthetic value *per se*, but on the assumption that nature is more valuable than development, then the preservationist is no further ahead for appealing to aesthetic considerations. The aesthetic assessments of the preservationist are 'morally charged', as Ned Hettinger puts it.[31]

The aesthetic preservationist faces a dilemma here. On the one hand, she can assess aesthetic value purely on aesthetic considerations. In principle, these considerations are capable of persuading sceptics that nature has greater value than the development that would replace it, but in practice they turn out not to favour nature as strongly as one would like, for the reasons discussed above. On the other hand, she can allow ethical judgements to play a role in shaping her aesthetic judgements. For example, she might hold that a natural area is aesthetically superior to urban sprawl in part because it is more natural, and what is natural is more valuable than what is artefactual. In that case, she can assert that nature generally has more aesthetic value than development, but her aesthetic assessments will cease to persuade the sceptic. For since the sceptic does not agree that nature has greater value, he will not generally find it more aesthetically appealing on this ethical basis. The dilemma means, in short, that, for the preservationist, the appeal to aesthetic value either fails to favour nature, or becomes a purely rhetorical device rather than a reason for accepting the preservationist position.

Let us consider the two horns of the dilemma in turn. If she chooses the first horn, the proponent of Aesthetic Preservation will aim to make hers a rationally persuasive case by spelling out some purely aesthetic reasons for thinking that, by and large, untouched nature is aesthetically superior to human development. An attempt at doing just this has been made by Janna Thompson.[32] She identifies four features of undomesticated nature that, she argues, make it by and large aesthetically superior to human development. These are: (1) magnificence and richness in detail; (2) the capacity to change or enhance our way of seeing the world; (3) cultural significance for those who experience it and (4) the capacity to put things in perspective. Thompson draws her list from reflection on the aesthetic value of artworks, and she explains the presence of its features in certain natural areas by way of analogies to artworks. Thus, just as a great work of architecture is magnificent and rich in detail – an inexhaustible feast for the senses, the intellect and the imagination – so too are natural areas such as the Grand Canyon. Just as some striking and unusual artworks – the paintings of Van Gogh, for instance – prompt us to see the world around us in a new way, so too can striking and unusual natural areas, such as the eucalyptus forests of south-eastern Australia. Some works of art, such as the masterworks of the Renaissance, provide a way of coming to appreciate a cultural tradition and our place in it, but so can some natural areas: Thompson gives the example of the Merri Creek grassland area, the ancestral home of the Koori aboriginal people in Australia. Like the works of da Vinci and Raphael, this grassland serves to connect certain people to their own cultural history. Finally, Thompson notes that great works of art force us to re-evaluate our basic values and 'pose a challenge to our way of thinking': analogously, nature can force us to put our daily activities into broader perspective. Nature, as Thompson puts it, 'exists as a refuge, or at least as a counterweight to the human-made world'.[33]

Thompson's list is not meant to be exhaustive: she admits that there might be other features in virtue of which nature is aesthetically superior to the human development that would supplant it. But she does claim that the respects that she cites are sufficient to show that 'the preference . . . for undomesticated nature can in many cases be justified'.[34]

Thompson's proposal is an attractive one, but the preservationist might also have concerns about the viability of Thompson's approach. First, some of her features seem to conflict with certain approaches to the aesthetics of nature. The proponent of the science-based approach to nature appreciation, for example, would probably be somewhat uneasy with taking cultural history to be a central aspect of the aesthetic value of natural things, as Thompson does. Second, it is unclear if some of the features that Thompson cites are truly indicative of *aesthetic* value. Consider the fourth factor, for instance: the capacity to put things into perspective. There is no doubt that helping us to put things into perspective is a valuable characteristic, but it does not seem clearly tied to the perceptual appearance of things in the way aesthetic qualities usually are. Plainly, lots of things can have this capacity without being aesthetically good at all: a slap in the face, for example, or a near death experience. This suggests that Thompson is unduly stretching the concept of the aesthetic in order to bolster the case for the aesthetic superiority of nature.

Perhaps a more important criticism is that the conception of Aesthetic Preservation that we can extract from Thompson's account is limited. Thompson acknowledges, for instance, that, on her account, not all natural areas will turn out to be aesthetically superior to human development. An unremarkable river bluff on the Mississippi will probably not possess any of the outstanding features on her list (perhaps only the fourth feature, if that). As such, an aesthetic argument for preserving it would be weak: in that case, perhaps a decent oil refinery or some urban sprawl would not really be much of an aesthetic loss, if any loss at all. This means that the utility of Aesthetic Preservation will be, in the final analysis, rather limited: it becomes a compelling argument for saving the so-called 'masterpieces' of nature: the Grand Canyon, or rare eucalyptus forests. But when it comes to preserving nature, these are the easy cases. This casts some doubt on whether Thompson's criteria really show that, as she says, 'the preference . . . for undomesticated nature can in many cases be justified'.

What about the second horn of the preservationist's dilemma? If she chooses this option, the preservationist can easily assert that nature has greater aesthetic value than development, but only because ethical considerations have infected her judgements of aesthetic value. This seems to leave the aesthetic superiority of nature worthless as a means of convincing people that nature has value, and so ought to be preserved. On this approach, nature's 'aesthetic superiority' is nothing more than a rhetorical device, a mirage that disguises the prior presumption of the value of nature over human development. If the preservationist is to justify preservation, and avoid simply begging the question against the sceptic, she must do the difficult work alluded to in the first section, and provide some other account of the non-practical value of nature. Doing so would save the preservationist view, but also seems to entail jettisoning aesthetic value, which apparently can now play no part in a rational preservationist argument. On this horn of the dilemma, in other words, preservation will no longer be Aesthetic Preservation.

Some philosophers, however, have suggested that this is overly pessimistic. They maintain that, even if it turns out that preservation rests on non-aesthetic considerations, and that aesthetic judgements are 'morally charged', aesthetic value can still make a useful contribution. The basic idea behind this view is the idea that, as Hettinger puts it, 'the language of aesthetics is more descriptive in comparison with the more prescriptive language of ethics'.[35] An ethical argument for the preservation of an endangered species, for example, will typically rely on ethical concepts such as rights, theoretical principles, such as the equal worth of all species, and ecological facts. But all of these are somewhat abstract. Aesthetic descriptions of such creatures can provide us with greater *specific* insight into the species that we are discussing, allowing us to, as Saito puts it, 'supplement our purely conceptual understanding of nature, and . . . strengthen our appreciation of nature's workings'.[36]

Hettinger gives the example of the campaign to save the Delhi Sands flower-loving fly, the only endangered fly species in the United States, by blocking the construction of a large industrial development in the fly's habitat. The fly's defenders relied on weighty moral arguments that were couched in the abstract language of rights and interests. They argued that the fly possessed value, despite its lack of utility for humans, and hence had the right to exist. But more effective than this argument, Hettinger suggests, were descriptions of the 'spectacular' aesthetic qualities of the fly, pointing out its unusual morphology and its odd, hummingbird-like manner of flying. Ultimately, these aesthetic qualities, in themselves, may not give us any grounds for saving the fly: they may be no more valuable, as aesthetic qualities, than the ones that a decent industrial plant would possess. However, through reflection on these aesthetic qualities, the strength of the ethical basis for choosing the fly – its inherent value and consequent right to exist – becomes clearer to us. As Hettinger puts it, such aesthetic experience makes possible 'a more informed assessment of the moral issues involved' and allows 'considerations to be entertained that disputants may not have noticed or appreciated'.[37] We might sum up this line of thought as the view that the aesthetic value of nature, even if it does not itself figure in the reasoning behind Aesthetic

Preservation, can still play a useful *heuristic* role in getting people to see that reasoning.

A sceptic might object here, however, that, in adopting this view, the preservationist is 'having her cake and eating it too': she gets to appeal to aesthetic value, even though she cannot show that it is a valid reason for preferring nature to human development. This, it might be said, is nothing different from the practice, discussed earlier in this chapter, of using pictures of aesthetically ruined natural areas to 'push people's buttons'. There is no doubt that, in virtue of their perceptual immediacy, aesthetic techniques can be more effective in swaying people to a course of action than dry facts and abstract moral concepts. But to so use them is to shift preservation away from a rational debate and towards a mere rhetorical contest. The preservationist can always simply accept the sceptic's objection with equanimity, of course, embracing the turn to rhetoric over reason. But to the extent that he does, philosophical analyses are no longer relevant to his project.

CHAPTER 8

NATURE IN THE GARDEN

Many philosophical studies of the aesthetics of nature, including our own so far, take the paradigm of nature appreciation to be an excursion into a wilderness area, such as a nature preserve. Such excursions offer us (at least in principle) nature on a grand scale, a largely non-human world where much of what happens takes place independently of human agency. But for many of us, much of the time, encounters with nature occur within the human world, and on a much smaller scale. In particular, for many of us, the most common location for our appreciation of nature is not wilderness at all, but the garden. Gardening is an enormously popular pastime, and has a very strong aesthetic dimension: a major part, though certainly not all, of the value of gardens comes from the aesthetic pleasure that they provide. It might seem, therefore, that in ignoring the experience of nature as it takes place in gardens we are, in fact, ignoring one of the most important ways in which people actually appreciate nature aesthetically.

To broaden our investigation, therefore, in this chapter we will explore the relationship between the aesthetic appreciation of gardens, particularly common domestic gardens, and the aesthetic appreciation of nature. In particular, we will focus on the degree to which nature can be said to be an element of such gardens, and the question of whether or not some degree of naturalness is essential to gardens.

THE GARDEN AS NATURE

If asked whether gardens contain nature, or natural things, many people would respond with an unhesitating 'yes'. Indeed, many of the ideas that one encounters frequently in discussions of gardens and gardening make this assumption. People often talk about large-scale public gardens, for example, as preserving or restoring nature in an otherwise artificial urban landscape; one also hears of the potential of smaller-scale domestic gardens to bring a 'bit of nature' to the beleaguered city dweller. The intuitive idea that gardens are natural is supported by the fact that gardens contrast sharply and vividly with the most visually prominent aspect of the human world: architecture. Unlike buildings, bridges and other architectural structures, gardens tend to be green, lacking in planar surfaces and sharp angles, and largely alive. This dramatic contrast can make it easy to assume that gardens and their contents belong to a category other than architecture: that they must be natural entities, rather than artificial ones.

Closer inspection of the nature and origin of gardens and their contents, however, shows that this would be a hasty judgement. For, if we return to our definition of nature as 'what takes place without the agency of man', we must admit that much of the garden is not natural. First, and perhaps most obviously, the layout and design of a garden, including the positioning of particular plants and the overall pattern formed by them, as well as the situation of additional elements such as paths and ponds, is often consciously chosen by the gardener, and hence unnatural. The size of particular plants in the garden, at any given time, is also often unnatural: by a judicious combination of pruning and fertilizing the gardener sculpts plants and hedges into desired forms. Indeed, even the mere growth of the plants can be somewhat unnatural, being brought about by the gardener's deliberate irrigation of an arid plot.[1] The presence of various sorts of animals in the garden, while sometimes natural, is often the result of contrivance, for which all manner of ingenious bird feeders and rodent repellents are deployed. And finally, the plants themselves as a rule owe their existence to prolonged and deliberate experiments in horticulture, employing techniques such as grafting, hybridization, and the like. Consider one of today's most common garden plants: the tulip.[2] The vast array of varieties available today is the product of centuries of laborious cultivation. Although there are wild varieties of tulip, these are highly uncommon in gardens. The process of 'artefactualization' of colour, shape and size that has been carried out on the tulip is the norm: most of today's commonly cultivated garden varieties differ greatly from their wild progenitors.

The upshot of all of this is that, despite looking quite different from humanly created architecture, gardens are, in fact, largely artefacts themselves. Rather than belonging to different categories, architecture and gardens can be grouped together. This is true even for what people sometimes call informal gardens. It is common to draw a distinction between formal gardens, associated with the French gardening tradition, and the informal garden, associated with eighteenth-century England.[3] The paradigm of a formal garden is the garden designed at Versailles for Louis XIV. Stephanie Ross sums up the character of this formal garden as 'rectilinear and architectural, unified by recurrent geometry and relentless axial symmetry'.[4] In the formal garden, the element of human contrivance is obvious and unabashed: the formal garden's affinity with architecture, as Ross's description indicates, is clear, despite the fact that it employs living materials (i.e. plants). In contrast, the informal garden popular in the English tradition downplays this element of human contrivance, rendering it less obvious. In the English informal garden, the particular aesthetic qualities associated with the picturesque – Uvedale Price's trio of irregularity, sudden variation and rough texture, for instance – were emphasized over mathematical regularities of form. But even though the informal garden employs a less mathematical, and so less *obviously* contrived design, the design may be no less contrived in reality. The variegated, flowing arrangements of the informal garden are often precisely planned and meticulously maintained. Further, the plants employed in the informal garden are often just as artefactual as those employed in formal gardens.

And, in truth, even though we are inclined to say that the informal garden looks more 'natural' than the formal garden, we still tacitly view it as an artefact. Imagine stumbling upon a typical informal garden in the middle of a completely natural wilderness. Your response to that sight would be very different from your response to the very same scene located in an urban backyard. A simple arrangement of pedestrian red geraniums might look plain and uninspired in the latter setting, but the very same row would jump out as incongruous and brilliant in the former. Such examples show that we do not really take informal gardens to be natural in the sense of 'occurring without the agency of man'. In that sense of the word, even informal gardens are relatively unnatural constructions.

We ought not to conclude from all of this, however, that there are absolutely no natural things in gardens, nor that there is absolutely nothing natural about gardens. That would be an overreaction. For, first of all, many of the materials employed in gardens are natural materials: dirt, stone and water, for instance. The construction of gardens often involves the extraction of these materials, their transport to a new location and the fashioning of them into certain sorts of unnatural structures, but the materials themselves remain natural in their composition and properties. Also, gardens often contain various living creatures, aside from plants, that are natural. The birds that frequent gardens for food and shelter, the squirrels and other animals that toil, often uninvited, in gardens, and the insects that live in the soil are all important elements. Natural also is the location or the environment of the garden itself: the air to which it is exposed, the wind that plays across it, the light and shade that, at different times of day, cover it and (to some extent) the moisture that ends up in it. And finally, all gardens are subject, to some degree, to uninvited alteration by the forces of nature. Not even the most diligent gardener can keep out all weeds, all blights, all invading animals, all of the time; nor can she stop the weather from doing what it will to her creation. As a result, the state of the garden at any given moment is likely to be in some degree natural, even if the garden's overall condition is largely due to conscious human action.[5]

What does this account of the naturalness of gardens tell us about the question with which we began? We wanted to know whether appreciating gardens could be considered a form of appreciating nature. Based on what has been said so far, our answer must be a deflationary one: to some, but a quite limited, degree. There are, as we have said, natural things in, and natural aspects to, gardens, and we can appreciate them by focusing upon these things and aspects, as opposed to the artefactual elements that are present along with them.[6] We can, for instance, attend to the stone employed in a garden wall by appreciating its natural qualities, such as its texture and colour, rather than its artefactual ones, such as its rectangular shape. We can also delight in those qualities of garden plants and animals that are natural: the colour of a maple tree's fall leaves, for example, or the plumage of birds. All of these instances could be counted as forms of aesthetically appreciating nature in the garden.

But, although these examples show that appreciating nature is a part of what we do in appreciating gardens, it remains only a part. Furthermore, that part is a relatively minor one in the sense that, were we to restrict our appreciation to these natural elements and aspects, we would be missing the bulk and core of what is there to be appreciated. Someone who aesthetically appraised a garden based only on the plumage of its birds, or the texture of its stone, for instance, while ignoring its layout and the highly non-natural colours, forms and arrangements of its cultivated plants, would be failing to make a fair assessment of the garden's aesthetic value. Gardens are so thoroughly artefactual, in short, that relatively little of the appreciation we carry out in them is an appreciation of nature.

It is perhaps important to note that this conclusion, in itself, does not diminish, in any way, the stature of the aesthetic appreciation of gardens. To say that the appreciation of gardens is not, to any great degree, an appreciation of nature is not to say that it is thereby defective, or less worthwhile, than the appreciation of nature. It is only to say that it is different from the appreciation of nature, and this is an insight worth having, given that gardens are often taken to be paradigms for the appreciation of nature. It suggests that, if we wish to think more correctly about the aesthetics of gardens, we would be better off viewing the garden not as nature, but as a form of art, one employing somewhat unusual media – rocks, plants, and so forth – that have certain natural features. Briefly pursing this idea of gardening as an art form will help us to further clarify the true importance of the garden's natural element.

THE GARDEN AS ART

If one takes the term 'art' in a certain sense, the claim that gardening is an art may seem bewildering. In one sense of the term, which we can distinguish as the 'capital A sense', 'Art' refers to certain kinds of objects or entities, such as paintings, sculpture, musical works and literature, that are produced by the creative activity of artists, displayed in art galleries, and interpreted and criticized by art critics. This is not very enlightening as a philosophical definition – it is circular, for one thing – but it does bring out the important fact that Art, in the capital A sense, typically involves certain sorts of people, places and activities: namely, artists, galleries, and critics. If this is the sense of 'Art' that one has in mind, one might well be puzzled by the idea that gardening is an Art form. For gardeners do not generally consider themselves to be artists, or group their creations with those of artists. Neither do we have garden critics in the sense that we have art critics. Experienced gardeners do sometimes write newspaper columns, but these typically involve dispensing practical advice rather than assessing the aesthetic merits of particular gardens. And finally, gardens, being highly non-portable, are not displayed in any special location, in the way that artworks are displayed in galleries. Perhaps the closest approximation to the experience of visiting an art gallery that we can find in the gardening world is the 'garden tour', where members of the public, or some group, are invited to visit various gardens. But again the difference between the artist and the gardener here is striking: whereas the artist stands or falls on the reception of his work at the gallery, serious gardeners need not participate in garden tours at all. Perhaps the most important difference of all is that the element of creativity that is so central in Art, at least in recent times, seems lacking in most gardening. Although gardening does have a creative element, it depends heavily on practical rules of 'composition' in a way that Art does not. While we can appreciate the creativity of gardeners, it is not considered a great fault in a garden that its design has been lifted from another, or that its plants are arranged according to a standard, time-honoured, plan. In short, the activity of gardening seems to bear little resemblance to those activities that we refer to as 'Art'.

Interestingly, this was not always the case. Stephanie Ross has documented how in eighteenth-century England, 'the art of gardening was considered every bit as noble as the arts of painting and poetry'.[7] Citing examples such as the garden at Stourhead, Pope's garden at Twickenham and the gardens at Stowe, Ross argues that eighteenth-century British gardens were interpreted much along the lines in which poems are interpreted, and were considered *bona fide* Artworks.[8] The gardens at Stourhead, for example, were designed as a circuit that took the visitor along a path meant to symbolize the journeys of Aeneas, legendary founder of Rome. Temples, statues, grottos and the shaping of the land itself were used to evoke mythological themes and give the garden a rich and complex meaning.

Whatever we want to say about these eighteenth-century gardens, however, it seems clear that today, gardens generally speaking are no longer Art. As Ross puts it, 'major artists do not make statements in this medium, and our sense of gardening's kinship to painting and poetry has been lost'.[9] Of course, a particular artist might decide to create an artwork that happens to be a garden: artists are notorious, after all, for turning anything into art. But this would be a very unusual case: virtually none of the enormous number of gardens currently in existence are considered Artworks, in the way that Stourhead and the other gardens mentioned above were. This seems to be the case not only for humble, small-scale amateur gardens, of the kind maintained by the average home-owner, but even for large-scale, professionally designed gardens.[10]

There is another sense of the term 'art', however, in which the claim that gardens are artworks is more plausible. On what we might call the 'lower case sense', 'art' means merely a practical skill or craft. This is the sense in which people speak of 'the art of navigation' or the 'fine art of collective bargaining'. These 'arts' (i.e. practical skills or crafts) do not involve the specific persons, places or activities associated with Art, nor do they necessarily eschew rules for creativity and originality, in the manner typical of Art. On the contrary, these arts often rely heavily on various practical rules. Taking 'art' in this sense, the claim that gardening is an art seems not only plausible, but enlightening, since there are clearly some arts whose aim is creating things of aesthetic value. Navigation and collective bargaining are not of this ilk, but arts such as gem-cutting, interior decoration and hair styling are. These are practical skills or crafts, in that they aim at producing a certain definite sort of thing, rather than something that is necessarily novel or original, or something to be thought of as 'Art'. But the sort of thing that these particular arts aim at producing is an aesthetically good sort of thing: a beautiful stone, a harmonious living room, an attractive hairstyle. Gardening fits nicely into this class of activities. In line with this, we might roughly define the concept of a garden as follows: the practical skill or craft of producing a certain kind of aesthetically pleasing object, making use of certain media, such as plants, rocks, soil, and so forth.

This definition, although partial and rough, allows us to address more precisely the issue that we raised in the previous section concerning the importance of the natural dimension of the garden. How, precisely, is naturalness related to the art of gardening? We observed that nature enters into the garden insofar as the media employed in gardening typically have certain natural aspects. Stone, for instance, is a natural substance and so it carries into the garden many, though not all, of its natural qualities. And the plants that are used in gardens, though often highly artefactualized, were derived from wild progenitors and so retain some natural traits and characteristics. But is this use of materials with a natural dimension merely an accidental feature of the art of gardening, or is it an essential one? In other words, does the practical craft of gardening really *require* that some natural qualities find their way into the garden, or, on the contrary, is it possible to conceive of a garden that lacks *any* such qualities, a garden that has no natural element at all?

The answer here may seem obvious: surely, if your craft involves using the particular media of plants, rocks and soil, then you really have no choice but to turn to nature as the source for those media. For many gardeners, at least most of the time, this is probably true in that the materials readily accessible in gardening stores and from local sources (quarries, for instance) may be mostly natural. But when we asked whether it is possible to have a garden with no natural materials, we were not interested in whether this was feasible in reality, or practical to do, but whether it is possible in principle. We wanted to know, that is, whether an arrangement of plants, rock and soil created without any natural element, if we could construct it, would still be a garden, as difficult or impractical as it might be for us to construct such a thing in reality.

In fact, constructing such a garden may not be as difficult or as far-fetched as it might seem at first glance. In the case of rock, landscaping companies commonly sell a wide variety of artificial stones, made from materials such as concrete, that mimic the form, colour and texture of natural stone. Likewise for soil: various processes have been designed for manufacturing artificial soils (sewage sludge, interestingly, is one source). Plants are a more difficult case: unlike rock or soil, artificial plants cannot yet be 'whipped up' through a synthetic manufacturing process. They must be bred laboriously from existing stock, which originates ultimately in wild plants. Because of this, the plants that we employ in our gardens, however artefactualized they become, tend to retain some natural aspects and properties. But it seems possible, in principle, for this limitation to be overcome also. It seems coherent to imagine horticulturists, through the use of sophisticated techniques for *in vitro* genetic recombination, designing and creating plants completely *de novo*. Similar scenarios involving animals have often been portrayed in science fiction: in the popular novel *Jurassic Park*, for example, scientists use genetic material to reconstruct living specimens of long extinct dinosaur species.[11] The creatures of *Jurassic Park* are, in fact, new members of a long extinct natural species, but we can easily imagine the scientists portrayed in the novel designing completely new 'dinosaurs' by recombining the genes of natural species, or even creating entirely new, 'unnatural' genetic sequences.[12] And it seems no more difficult to imagine horticulture advancing to a similar point, where the creation of living plants could be made into a completely artificial process. The question of nature's place in the garden, then, comes down to this: in the scenario where we use technology to create an arrangement of rocks, soil and plants that possesses all of the general features of a garden, but *without any natural element at all*, have we failed to produce a genuine garden?

IS NATURE ESSENTIAL TO THE GARDEN?

Philosophical opinion, it would seem, is divided on this question. Stephanie Ross says 'no': 'most but not all gardens contain natural materials'.[13] Other philosophers, apparently, would say 'yes'. Mara Miller, for example, defines 'garden' as 'any purposeful arrangement of natural objects (such as sand, water, plants, rocks, etc.) with exposure to the sky or open air, in which the form is not fully accounted for by purely practical considerations such as convenience'.[14] If we take 'natural' here as what takes place without the agency of man, then Miller's definition simply does not apply to the garden we imagined at the end of the previous section. For that garden, while it is an arrangement of sand, water, plants, rocks, and so forth, is an arrangement of wholly artefactual objects. Miller's discussion does not take up this issue, however, and so fails to provide us with a justification for the view, apparently implicit in her definition, that naturalness, to some degree, is essential to the garden.[15] What sort of justification might be provided here?

One consideration that might incline us to the view that some degree of naturalness is essential to the garden is the existence of particular kinds of artificial constructions that we would intuitively resist describing as gardens. Consider, for instance, a virtual garden. Virtual reality is a form of computer technology designed to replicate the experience of certain places, events or objects in the absence of those places, events and objects. Thus virtual reality can be used to replicate the experience of flying a plane, even though the person having the experience is not in a plane at all, but sitting in a chair in a basement. Various sorts of sensory prosthetics, such as eyepieces, ear phones, and so forth, can be used to create these virtual experiences, and if they are sophisticated enough, the virtual experiences may be indistinguishable from the real thing. We can easily imagine such technology being used to generate the experience of being in a garden, in the absence of an actual garden. A person employing this technology could smell the flowers, feel the wind, see the arrangements of plants and perhaps even move around, just as if she were in a garden.[16] But many of us would hesitate to describe the object experienced here as a garden. Rather, one might argue, what we have is an image, or a simulacrum, of a garden, albeit a very sophisticated one.

A less extreme example, but along the same lines, is that of the plastic garden. Imagine an arrangement of objects that look just like plants, but are not alive. The biologist E.O. Wilson describes such a garden:

> Visualize a beautiful and peaceful world, where the horizon is rimmed by snowy peaks reaching into a perfect sky. In the central valley, waterfalls tumble down the faces of steep cliffs into a crystalline lake. . . . Artisans have worked across the terrain below to create a replica of one of Earth's landscape treasures, perhaps a formal garden from late eighteenth-century England, or the Garden of the Golden Pavilion at Kyoto, marked by an exquisite balance of water, copse, and trail. The setting is the most pleasing that human

imagination can devise. Except for one thing – it contains no life whatsoever. This world has always been dead. The vegetation of the garden is artificial, shaped from plastic and colored by master craftsmen down to the last blade and stem . . . the only sounds are the broken rhythms of the falling water and an occasional whisper of wind through the plastic trees.[17]

Wilson's example is large-scale and fanciful, but it has a small-scale and real world analogue: the phenomenon of 'no grow' gardens, which contain only plastic trees and plants, or even no plants at all.[18] Usually for reasons of convenience, home-owners remove the plants from their properties and replace them with plastic imitations. But are these locales then really gardens? Again, many will have the intuition that they are not, viewing it as more accurate to describe them as mere simulations or imitations of gardens. If this reading of the virtual and plastic 'garden' cases is correct, then they might be taken to support the notion that naturalness is essential to the garden: what prevents these entities from being gardens, it might be argued, is their lacking some element of naturalness.

However, not everyone would agree with this reading of these cases. Ross, for instance, describes an unusual garden designed by Clifford Davis, consisting of rubber ducks, plastic daisies and Astroturf.[19] Ross seems happy describing this as 'a garden'; in fact, she further imagines an avant-garde sort of garden that dispenses with plants altogether, containing only trellises.[20] This garden, even more blatantly than Davis's garden, would be wholly unnatural. Yet, she is willing to consider it a garden. Furthermore, our linguistic practices seem to support the position taken by Ross here, that plastic gardens can be real gardens: Wilson describes his imaginary setting using the word 'garden', after all, and the phrase 'no grow garden' is applied to the arrays of fake plants mentioned above. And if people commonly use the term 'garden' to refer to such arrangements of plastic objects, without creating confusion or obscurity, shouldn't we take this as evidence that our concept of the garden is broad enough to include such items?

This is a strong consideration, but I think that it is nonetheless mistaken to conclude that assemblages of plastic plants are actually gardens. The reason is that the linguistic evidence that supports this view is, I think, not genuine but only apparent. The root of the problem is that there are actually two importantly distinct senses of the word 'garden' in English. One is the sense which we have been using so far, the sense which describes a certain sort of assemblage of entities (plants, soil, rocks, and so on). The other sense is that used simply to designate a particular area, typically one immediately adjacent to a house or some similar building.[21] In this sense, 'garden' simply refers to a certain plot of land, implying nothing about its contents. In this sense, it is perfectly coherent to speak of 'plastic gardens', for these entities are plots of land adjacent to a building. But our describing them as gardens in this sense is not evidence that they are also gardens *in the other sense* of that term, the sense to which we have been appealing so far in our discussion.

A useful way to see the difference between these two senses of 'garden' is to note that only the latter is connected to the verb form 'gardening'. A paved area behind one's house can be a garden in the 'plot of land adjacent to a building' sense, but we cannot sensibly speak about gardening in relation to it. One can work on, or improve, the paved area behind one's house, to be sure – by washing or painting it, for example – but no one would describe this activity as 'gardening'. Something similar is true for plastic gardens: a stand of urethane trees could be truly described as one's 'garden', in the 'plot of land adjacent to a building' sense, but one could not describe working on that stand, by repainting the trees, for example, or moving them into different positions, as 'gardening'. This kind of activity has a much greater affinity with activities like the construction of mechanical trains, or model-building, than it has with the activity of gardening. In sum, the word 'garden' expresses distinct concepts when used in the 'plot of land adjacent to a building' sense, and when used in the 'gardening sense'. Consequently, we cannot conclude, simply from the application of the word 'garden' to some thing, that the concept that we are interested in – that of a garden in the gardening sense – really applies to that thing. This point is even clearer in the case of virtual gardens: the construction and manipulation of such 'spaces', through the manipulation of a computer for instance, seems clearly not a form of gardening, however we might ultimately decide to classify it.

If this line of thought is correct, then our potential justification for the claim that a natural element is essential in gardens stands: plastic and virtual 'gardens' are not truly gardens, and this, we might conclude, is due to their lacking any natural element.

This conclusion would be hasty, however, for a different interpretation of these cases is also possible. It may be that plastic and virtual 'gardens' lack some other feature that is essential to the garden, and that *this* deficiency is what disqualifies them as genuine gardens. If this is the case, then naturalness may not be essential to the garden after all. And, in fact, there is a plausible alternative candidate for such an essential quality in gardens: namely, containing life.

The cultivation of living things is obviously an important dimension of the art of gardening; folksy discussions of the virtues of gardening often take up the nurturing and care that it involves, for instance. But, one might argue, the role of biological life in gardening is even deeper than this: a practice that did not involve living organisms, no matter how much it resembled gardening in other respects, would not be gardening. It would be something else.[22] If this claim is true, then the examples of the virtual and plastic 'gardens' described above are readily explicable: neither includes real living organisms, but only the illusion or imitation of such organisms. Thus, neither is a garden. Nothing about these examples, then, suggests that naturalness is essential in gardens. This claim, in other words, undercuts one reason for thinking that a completely artefactual garden is impossible.

The viability of the claim that gardens can never be entirely non-living is clouded by a tendency to conflate the concepts *unnatural* and *non-living*. When people talk about unnatural things, works of human contrivance, it is often tacitly assumed that these are non-living things. Wilson, for example, in critiquing the hypothetical world that he describes, says that 'artifacts are incomparably poorer than the life they are designed to mimic'.[23] By this he means that they lack certain features of living things: complexity and spontaneity, for instance. But although this is true of most artefacts, it is not necessarily the case, for living things can be artefacts too: consider the example of genetically engineered plants and animals mentioned earlier, for instance. The concept of being alive, in other words, is logically independent of the concept of being an artefact. Sometimes, the tacit assumption that artefacts are non-living is harmless, as it is in Wilson's discussion, where he is really only concerned with the subset of artefacts that are non-living.[24] But in other cases, it can generate confusion about the importance of naturalness.

For example, in a well-known passage of his *Critique of the Power of Judgement*, Kant makes the following claim about the lover of natural beauty:

> If someone had secretly deceived this lover of the beautiful and had planted artificial flowers (which can be manufactured to look entirely similar to natural ones) or had placed artfully carved birds on the twigs of trees, and he then discovered this deception, the

immediate interest that he had previously taken in it would immediately disappear . . .[25]

Kant takes this example to fit with the conclusion that 'the thought that
nature has produced that beauty . . . on this alone is grounded the immediate interest that one takes in it'.[26] And from the response to the fake
flowers and the carved birds that is described in this passage, one might
easily conclude that naturalness in such things is essential for an immediate interest in their beauty. But this would be a hasty inference, because
carved birds and artificial flowers are also non-living things. One might
as well conclude, on the basis of Kant's example alone, that it is on the
thought that these are alive, rather than produced by nature, on which our
immediate interest in their beauty is grounded.[27] In that case, naturalness
would not be essential to the phenomenon in question.

The same cautionary point applies to our examples of virtual and
plastic 'gardens'. Their failure as gardens might be due to their lack of
life, rather than their lack of naturalness. But is this the case? Can we
claim that naturalness is, after all, not essential to the garden? I believe
that we can. Consider again the completely unnatural garden imagined at
the end of the previous section: the use of technology to create an arrangement of rocks, soil and plants that possesses all of the typical features of
a garden, but *without any natural element at all*. It seems reasonable to
describe this arrangement as a garden, since there is no strain in describing the creation and maintenance of such an arrangement as gardening.
Imagine, for example, that humans succeed in colonizing another planet,
but for logistical reasons are unable to bring any natural materials to their
new home. Finding the climate hostile, the colonists are forced to use
advanced technology to create artificial soil and stone, and even entirely
novel plants, designed for their new planet's particular environs. Using
these, they create assemblages that resemble, in their general structure,
our own gardens. I take it that the most natural thing to say about these
colonists is that they are gardening. If this is correct, then naturalness is
indeed completely accidental to the craft of gardening.

If we say this, of course, we will not deny that most, perhaps all, extant
gardens have some natural aspects or elements, nor that, in certain cases,
these aspects or elements are important and substantial. But we will
maintain that nature comes into the garden only accidentally, in virtue of
the fact that presently, the materials used in gardening, especially living
plants, need to be drawn ultimately from nature, and thus retain some
natural aspects. And we will aver that, if completely artefactual gardens

are ever constructed, as in our futuristic colonization scenario, for instance, such gardens will have as firm a claim to being gardens as those existing today, so long as they contain living organisms. If and when that day comes, nature and gardening, held together so long only by the limitations of our technology, will then come apart completely, and perhaps, for good.

CHAPTER 9

ART IN NATURE

In the previous chapter, we extended our investigation of the aesthetic appreciation of nature beyond the usual paradigm case of appreciating wilderness, by taking up the appreciation of nature in a physical part of the human world: the garden. In this final chapter, we will continue in this direction by considering the appreciation of nature in the context of a more conceptual dimension of the human world: art.[1] As noted in the last chapter, art and gardening have long since parted company in the Western world. But this does not mean that art has left nature behind. One of the most innovative and interesting branches of contemporary art, environmental art, focuses upon nature and the natural environment. Works in this genre draw upon natural materials and phenomena, and present them to us for appreciation in the context of a creative work by the artist.

In considering this form of nature appreciation, we will focus on two issues. The first is the precise sort of involvement of nature in environmental art. To what extent is nature a part of environmental artworks, and can we really say that we are appreciating nature when we appraise these works? The second issue, which we will treat at greater length, is whether there is something unethical about the treatment of nature involved in the creation of environmental artworks. This second issue has been much discussed by philosophers, and in considering it, we will confront, a final time, a concern that has run throughout much of our discussion in this book: the connection between aesthetic appreciation and our ethical relationships with the natural world.

ENVIRONMENTAL ART: AN AFFRONT TO NATURE?

Environmental art is a genre of recent vintage, having originated in the 1960s. Nonetheless, it includes a wide variety of works. At one extreme, we find the most vivid examples of the genre: large-scale manipulations of natural sites, such as the 'earthworks' of artists like Michael Heizer and Robert Smithson. Heizer's *Double Negative* (1969–70) consists of two massive rectangular cuts in the top of a desert mesa in southern Nevada. These cuts are 50 feet deep, 30 feet wide and over 1,500 feet long, and the work was constructed using bulldozers and dynamite. One of Smithson's best-known pieces is a work known as *Spiral Jetty* (1970). As the name suggests, the work consists of a coil-shaped jetty, 1,500 feet long, composed of rock and earth, and situated in Utah's Great Salt Lake. For a period of time rising water levels in the lake rendered it invisible from the shoreline, although it was visible from the air. Recently, a drop in water levels has made it visible again.[2]

The earthworks of Heizer and Smithson are on an enormous scale, involving dramatic interventions in nature. But not all environmental artworks are of this type. Alan Sonfist's work *Time Landscape* (1965) involved the artist simply allowing a city block in New York City to revert to its natural state. And moving still further from the works of Heizer and Smithson, we find small-scale and unobtrusive works that incorporate natural materials and sites, such as certain works by the contemporary British artist Andy Goldsworthy. His descriptively titled work *Sycamore Leaves Stitched Together* (1987), for example, consists of an arrangement of naturally occurring objects situated in a more or less undisturbed natural site. Other of his works involve placing leaves on streams, stacking stones on top of one another and turning a small pool of water red by rubbing stones together to release natural pigment into the water.

The environmental artworks described above differ greatly in their employment of nature. What can we say, in general, about the role of nature in environmental art? In all of these works, nature is a part of the work in two important senses.[3] First, nature is a part of the medium employed by the artist, in some substantial sense.[4] For example, Goldsworthy's *Sycamore Leaves* is made out of leaves and situated in a forest, and *Spiral Jetty* is made out of stone and situated in a lake. In all of the works described above, the fact that natural materials and sites are employed in the work is essential to the work. These specific works could not have been made from some synthetic materials, and cannot be moved to some different site. Second, natural materials are not only a crucial element of the artwork's medium, they are also a part of its content. Thus, works such as *Sycamore Leaves* and *Spiral Jetty* do not simply happen to be made of natural materials: they are, in part, about those natural materials. That is, acknowledging the natural element of an environmental artwork is vital for understanding the meaning of the work.

In virtue of these two features, then, all of the works on our list, despite their great differences, can be classed within the broad category of environmental art.

This categorization of environmental art presents an interesting contrast with gardens. As we saw in the previous chapter, it is arguable that, even though they often employ natural materials and have natural aspects, gardens are not essentially natural. Gardening could be carried out without the use of nature at all. But this is not the case for environmental art. Environmental art is defined as art that uses nature as a part of its medium, to express something about nature. As such, the natural elements that figure in these works are integral to their being environmental art. In appreciating works in this genre, we necessarily appreciate various natural forces and objects, though always within the context of the artwork.

This answers the first question raised at the start of this chapter, namely: 'To what extent is nature a part of environmental art?' But it also raises our second question: Is there something unethical about the treatment of nature in the creation of environmental artworks? Environmental art essentially involves the artist intervening in nature, and appropriating it for artistic purposes. If one accepts that, in general, our treatment of nature merits ethical consideration, we must ask whether the treatment of nature involved in the creation of environmental art is ethically acceptable or not. One obvious reason for thinking that a particular way of treating nature is unethical would be its causing serious ecological harm to nature. These concerns may be acute with some environmental artworks, such as those of Smithson and Heizer, and less so for others (many of Goldsworthy's works, for instance, have little or no environmental impact, in this sense). But environmental art also raises a different, and more philosophically interesting ethical worry, which is whether the creation of environmental art constitutes an aesthetic affront to nature.[5]

The general idea behind the notion of an aesthetic affront is an insult, indignity, or slight to X that is based on interference with the aesthetic qualities of X. As such, an aesthetic affront to nature is an ethically problematic behaviour towards a natural site, but one different from more typically cited kinds of ethically problematic behaviours towards such sites, such as causing serious ecological harm. The creation of environmental art is thought to involve an aesthetic affront to nature in virtue of two facts. First, prior to the intervention of the artist, nature possesses a set of aesthetic qualities, which it has as the natural thing it is. A mountain face might look rugged and imposing, for instance; if so, this is an aesthetic quality it has as a natural thing. Second, in creating environmental art, the artist converts nature to art, thereby changing its aesthetic qualities. As an analogy, Allen Carlson offers Duchamp's conversion of a copy of the *Mona Lisa* into his Dadaist work, *L.H.O.O.Q.* (1919), by adding a moustache and goatee.[6] This conversion involved altering the aesthetic qualities of the object in question: after its conversion into a Dadaist work, the object acquired aesthetic qualities, such as looking discordant or ironic, which it lacked before the conversion. The same sort of aesthetic transformation occurs in the creation of environmental art. As Carlson puts it, the conversion of nature into an artwork comes at a 'cost to [nature's] aesthetic qualities', as those qualities are destroyed, or at least obscured, by the new aesthetic qualities that are imposed on the object.[7]

Together, these facts about environmental art raise the question of whether it is an aesthetic affront to nature. For replacing the aesthetic qualities of an object with a different set of aesthetic qualities, through a conversion of the object into an artwork, might be construed as an insult, indignity, or slight to the aesthetic character of the original object. Why is this? Consider again Duchamp's *L.H.O.O.Q.* Since Duchamp in fact used a copy of the *Mona Lisa*, this work is not an apt analogy for the creation of environmental art, which uses actual nature, not an imitation of it.[8] So let us imagine a visually indiscernible work, created in the same way by Duchamp, but using the original *Mona Lisa*: call this work *L.H.O.O.Q.**.[9] In creating *L.H.O.O.Q.**, Duchamp would clearly have been implicitly affronting the original work. This is the case insofar as this action would manifest the attitude that the *Mona Lisa* is not worthy of continued unmolested existence, since it is deemed necessary to replace it with something else: namely, *L.H.O.O.Q.**. It is important to note that this would be the case even if the interference with the aesthetic qualities of the original work, the *Mona Lisa*, was temporary. As Carlson puts it, 'had Duchamp penciled the mustache and goatee on the *Mona Lisa* and erased it after a few days, he would yet have accomplished his affront to the work'.[10] For this action would still manifest the attitude that the *Mona Lisa* is not worthy of continued unmolested existence, since it is deemed necessary to replace it (temporarily) with something else: namely, *L.H.O.O.Q.**. Since subsequent removal of the physical traces of the act of creating *L.H.O.O.Q.** does not change this fact, this action remains an affront to the original work of art.

The creation of an environmental artwork, however, can be construed in the same fashion: as manifesting the attitude that the original natural object is not worthy of continued unmolested existence, since it is deemed necessary to replace it with something else (the environmental artwork). Further, this would be the case even when the environmental artwork itself is temporary in nature, being later removed by the artist or by natural process.[11] In this manner, the creation of environmental art might be said to constitute an aesthetic affront, slight, or indignity to nature.

DEFENDING ENVIRONMENTAL ART

Recently, a number of philosophers have taken issue with the claim that environmental art constitutes an aesthetic affront to nature. In this section, we will consider one response to this claim: the idea that some environmental art has a special character that makes it immune to the effrontery charge.[12] The philosophers who advance this response are willing to concede that some environmental artworks, some of Heizer's earthworks, for instance, are aesthetic affronts to nature.[13] They point out, however, the extreme nature of these works, and note that, in other cases, it is less clear that an aesthetic affront has been committed. In general, philosophers who are critical of the charge of effrontery point to three circumstances that mitigate the charge.

The first factor is the presence of a certain attitude towards nature, as an artistic 'material', or 'medium', on the part of environmental artists. This attitude is described by Emily Brady as the displaying of 'a form of aesthetic regard' for nature.[14] In displaying this attitude, the artist pays careful attention to the original aesthetic value of nature, and develops the environmental artwork in a way that acknowledges and relates to that value. As an example of this attitude, Brady cites Goldsworthy's works, which often employ natural materials and incorporate natural forces, such as the heat of the sun or the forces of wind and tide. In art such as Goldsworthy's, she writes, 'the artist's role becomes one of enabling or increasing attentiveness to nature's qualities by pointing to them, highlighting them and working with them creatively. In these ways, ephemeral artworks show aesthetic regard for nature.'[15] This attitude of aesthetic regard for nature is a far cry, Brady notes, from the 'macho aggression' evident in certain of Heizer's works.[16] Unlike the latter, Goldsworthy does not obliterate nature's aesthetic qualities; rather, his works can even be said to enhance those qualities. Perhaps we may attend more closely to the look of leaves or to the subtle effects of the forces of wind and tide after seeing one of Goldsworthy's works, for instance.

A second factor thought to mitigate the charge of effrontery is the aesthetic improvement that environmental art can bring about: environmental artworks can be aesthetically valuable, more valuable, in some cases, than the undisturbed natural sites in which they are situated. The general idea here is to point to a positive feature of the creation of environmental art, a feature that, in fact, is positive for nature as well as for ourselves, since it is the natural site that is aesthetically improved through the creation of the artwork.[17] Philosophers who dispute the charge of effrontery do not appeal to this factor very explicitly, but their discussions do suggest that it ought to play a role in this debate.[18] Aesthetic improvement of nature is most compelling when added to the previous factor: aesthetic regard for nature. Some of Goldsworthy's works, for example, seem to improve upon nature's aesthetic character in a way that incorporates nature's own aesthetic qualities. *Sycamore Leaves*, for example, creates an arrangement that does not exist in nature, but uses nature's own forms and materials. The aesthetic power of this arrangement, a vivid and bold tableau of colour and form, seems to be a benefit that we ought to weigh against the 'cost' to nature's original aesthetic qualities. As such, it seems relevant to assessing the charge of effrontery.

The third mitigating factor is also a benefit that the creation of environmental art brings to nature. But rather than an aesthetic benefit, it consists in the wider ecological benefit that environmental artworks may secure. Some environmental artists claim to be motivated by ecological concerns, and portray their environmental art as a means for advancing an environmentalist agenda. It could do so insofar as the modification of nature involved in such works forces the viewer to attend more closely to the human–nature relationship. Above I alluded to Goldsworthy's *Red Pool, Scaur River, Dumfriesshire* (1994–5); this work presents us with a starkly artificial-looking scene, even though the alteration here has been performed using natural materials. Its strange and subtle mingling of artifice and nature invites meditation on the relationship between the human and natural worlds.[19] In virtue of the particular way in which it employs nature as its medium, Lintott describes environmental art as having 'the potential to unite human beings in the inclusive and progressive mindset of environmentalism'.[20]

The existence of these three mitigating factors suggests that the original charge against environmental art, that it constitutes an aesthetic affront to nature, was overblown. Though a handful of extreme cases may deserve the epithet of 'affront', the conversion of nature into art can be done in a manner that shows regard for nature's own aesthetic qualities, that improves on the aesthetic value of the environment, and that is environmentally beneficial *for nature*. On the line of thought laid out by the critics of the effrontery charge, we ought to consider these nuances in the human/nature relationship. Once we do, we will see that the human–nature relationship evident in environmental art is not accurately described by saying that the artist has affronted nature.

Before critically assessing this response to the effrontery charge, we can reinforce it by considering again the analogy of Duchamp's *L.H.O.O.Q.**. Duchamp's action in creating this work would be a clear affront to the aesthetic qualities of the *Mona Lisa*. But notice that in creating *L.H.O.O.Q.**, Duchamp would not have improved the aesthetic qualities of the *Mona Lisa*, engaged with it in a way that respected its extant aesthetic qualities, or benefited it in the long run. In short, the creation of *L.H.O.O.Q.**, while clearly an aesthetic affront, would embody none of the mitigating features that are present in many cases of environmental art, such as Goldsworthy's works. *L.H.O.O.Q.** is more like the extreme works of Heizer than it is like the latter works. This reinforces the idea that the case against environmental art has been hastily generalized.

In response to this argument, the proponent of the effrontery charge will insist that it is not clear that the considerations at issue here are, in fact, sufficient to deflect the charge that, in general, environmental artworks are aesthetic affronts to nature. To see this, consider the following analogy. I come over to your house for a visit. While you pour some drinks in the kitchen, I wait in the living room. As I wait, I proceed to rearrange the pillows, move the furniture around, rearrange the paintings hanging on your walls, and things of this nature. In other words, I 'gussy up' your living room a bit. This seems to be a clear case of an aesthetic affront. It is so insofar as the action manifests the attitude that what is there originally in your living room is not worthy of continued unmolested existence, since it was deemed necessary to replace it with something else.

This analogy is informative for the case of environmental art because the response to the charge of effrontery described above involves admitting that the casual obliteration of nature's aesthetic qualities is effrontery, but then distinguishing a milder treatment of nature that, because of the mitigating factors mentioned, falls short of effrontery. But although this milder treatment of nature preserves or enhances the aesthetic character of nature, to some degree or another, instead of merely obliterating it, this treatment is also ethically problematic. This is so insofar as it can be thought of, essentially, as a kind of gussying up of nature. And, as the analogy of the living room shows, it is not only the wholesale obliteration of aesthetic qualities that can constitute an aesthetic affront; the milder act of gussying up can be an aesthetic affront as well.

Further, note that none of mitigating factors appealed to for environmental art are sufficient to defeat the charge of aesthetic effrontery in the case of the living room. My gussying up of your living room constitutes an affront even if it is done in a manner that is respectful of your living room's own aesthetic qualities, that improves on the aesthetic value of the room, and that is beneficial *for your living room*. For instance, in gussying up your living room I might recognize and attend to some of its original aesthetic qualities, and merely try to 'enhance' them. I might note the fine harmony of your furniture and some of your paintings, for instance, and try to bring this out a little more through a judicious repositioning of the sofa. Further, I might indeed succeed in this: I might be an interior designer with a better eye for these things, or perhaps you have simply failed to devote sufficient attention to the matter. Finally, my gussying up your living room might even be of positive benefit to it in the long run: you and your guests might enjoy it more. Perhaps my adjustments even increase the resale value of your home. However these things may be, it seems to me that my gussying up your living room remains an aesthetic affront. It is so insofar as it manifests the attitude that what is there originally is not worthy of continued unmolested existence, since it is deemed necessary to replace it with something else.

The same is true, seemingly, of the three mitigating factors when appealed to in the case of environmental art: they do not suffice to defeat the charge of aesthetic effrontery there either. The fact that environmental artworks preserve or even enhance the aesthetic qualities of nature does not change the fact that such works manifest the attitude that what is there originally is not worthy of continued unmolested existence. If it were worthy of such existence, the artwork in question would not have been created. The fact that the artist improves on the aesthetic quality of nature is similarly irrelevant: regardless of how much better the site becomes, the actions manifest the attitude that what is there originally is not worthy of continued unmolested existence. And finally, the fact that the creation of environmental art is good for our awareness of environmental issues, and ultimately for the environment itself, in the long run, also fails to change the fact that such interventions manifest the attitude that what is there originally is not worthy of continued unmolested existence, since it was deemed necessary to replace it with something else.

This last point deserves further consideration, for it might be thought that the creation of environmental art does not actually manifest this attitude, at least on the artist's part. It might be thought that the artist works the land reluctantly, doing so only as a last resort, to save it from destruction by the human race in general. If so, then the gussying up of nature characteristic of environmental art might be thought *not* to constitute an affront to nature.

Although some environmental artists profess a concern with the well-being of nature, one could certainly dispute the general claim that they work the land reluctantly, doing so only to save it from destruction at the hands of the human race in general. One might also dispute the notion that it is really necessary to resort to environmental art in order to save nature from destruction.[21] But even if these claims turned out to be true, this would not undermine the claim that what environmental artists do is an aesthetic affront to nature. For an affront against X can be intended to serve the interests of X; indeed, it may be necessary for the very survival of X.

Consider, for example, the well-intentioned Europeans who, after initial contacts with indigenous people in the New World, captured individuals from those peoples and toured them through the capitals of Europe in a bid to increase awareness of their desperate plight. Though it certainly was not always so, such treatment may have been genuinely intended to help indigenous peoples; in some cases, it may even have worked. Nonetheless, parading these individuals in this way was an indignity, an affront, to them. The fact that Europeans, on the whole, were sufficiently ignorant and apathetic for such degrading measures to be necessary does nothing whatever to mitigate this fact. Analogously, the fact that people in our time are so ignorant and apathetic about nature that it takes a glowing red pool of water to interest them in it does nothing to mitigate the effrontery of such frumpery. To excuse the effrontery of environmental art in this way would be to deny one wrong simply because of the existence of a larger, more pervasive one.

It may be useful to return to the analogy with art here. As mentioned above, cases like *L.H.O.O.Q.** do not provide a good analogy for the discussion of environmental art. Being an irreverent, insensitive and extreme treatment, its genesis seems not to resemble the ways in which many artists, such as Goldsworthy, work the land. But the ways in which such artists do work the land also constitute a form of aesthetic effrontery, a form not inaptly described as 'gussying up nature'. If we want an analogy with the case of art, we ought to think of the gussying up of an artistic masterpiece: an 'updating' of the *Mona Lisa* that lovingly adds some new patches of colour here and there (hoping to draw further attention to the wonderful rendering of the mouth, perhaps), inserts a few items of additional interest into the background, and so on, all in the interests of enhancing the work's continued interest to contemporary viewers, and hence, its survival as an artwork. Such an updating might be well-intentioned, aesthetically successful and perhaps even necessary in a barbaric age. But none of that would make it any less an indignity to the work of art.

IS THE EFFRONTERY CHARGE COHERENT?

The line of thought spelled out in the previous section represents one possible way of responding to the charge of effrontery. That line of thought accepts the cogency, in principle, of aesthetic affronts to nature, but argues that, in reality, most environmental artworks are not of this kind. It is also possible to make a different response to the effrontery charge, however, by denying the cogency of the whole idea of an aesthetic affront to nature. In this section, we examine two variations on this approach.

The first of these is the claim that the very idea of affronting nature is logically incoherent: the notion of an affront simply is not applicable to non-human things, such as the natural entities and sites that are altered in the creation of environmental art. This claim is not the claim that non-human things cannot be affronted *aesthetically*, but the stronger claim that they cannot be affronted at all. The claim is this stronger one since it is based on a view concerning the logic of the notion of an affront. Roughly, that view is that there is a logical connection between the notion of certain actions affronting (or insulting, or offering an indignity to) X and the notion that X can think, feel and respond to those actions in some way. This being the case, although one can, through one's words or actions, affront or insult a person, it does not make sense to speak of someone affronting a forest, or committing an indignity against a desert mesa.

In support of this view, one might point out that there are some concepts, apart from the concept of an affront, whose application surely does presuppose the mental capacities characteristic of persons. The notion of forming a contract with X, for example, presupposes that X is capable of thinking and exercising some form of conscious control over its actions.

For this reason, it does not make sense to talk of someone forming a contract with a mountain or a lake. This is shown by the fact that it would be inane to criticize a mountain that had undergone a landslide for 'breaking some contract' I had with it. If the notion of 'insulting' is like the notion of 'forming a contract', in this regard, then, since non-human entities such as forests, lakes and mesas are incapable of thinking, feeling and responding in a literal sense, we cannot sensibly say that human actions are capable of affronting those entities. The most we could sensibly say is that these actions affront, in an indirect way, other persons who care about these non-human entities.

There is clearly something compelling about this line of reasoning. However, it is not clear that it can provide a satisfactory response to the charge of effrontery. The line of reasoning is compelling because it certainly does hold for *some* forms of insult or effrontery. Consider the following insults: 'You're a failure' and 'You're shallow'. Directing these statements at a person can be a way of insulting or slighting him. But it makes no sense to try to insult a non-human entity, a stone, say, or a mesa, in this way. Pronouncing a stone a failure, or shallow, is nonsensical because stones cannot think, feel or act intentionally: they cannot attempt to do anything, and hence cannot be said to have carried off the things they have tried to do well or poorly. So the present response to the effrontery charge is certainly correct in holding that some forms of effrontery are logically connected to the possession of mental capacities characteristic of persons.

However, it does not follow that *all* forms of effrontery are logically connected to the possession of mental capacities characteristic of persons. And the kind of affront that we sketched in the first section of this chapter, in outlining the charge of effrontery against environmental art, is of this type. According to that sketch, we affront X if our actions towards X manifest the attitude that X is not worthy of continued unmolested existence, since it is deemed necessary to replace it with something else. We might think of this as an action's manifesting a kind of disregard, disrespect or contempt for an autonomous thing: a sort of undue 'messing with' it. Nothing in the logic of this conception of an affront requires the thing affronted to possess the capacity to think, feel or act intentionally. That our actions towards the thing in question satisfy the above condition (i.e. manifest a particular sort of disregard) is sufficient to make our action an affront to it, whatever its particular nature happens to be.

Even if this is the case, however, there is another way of questioning the cogency of the charge of effrontery. Instead of focusing on the logical coherence of the idea of affronting nature, we might focus on the conse-quences of the charge of effrontery. The idea here is that, even if it could be shown that the notion of an affront can, in principle, be applied to non-sentient nature, the claim that environmental art is an aesthetic affront to nature would commit us to saying that such benign actions such as farming and building homes are also aesthetic affronts to nature, which is absurd.

The reasoning behind this idea is as follows. In order to survive, there are various interventions that we must make in the natural environment: we need food, water and shelter, for instance. Obtaining any of these requires that we take the attitude that nature, as it is, needs to be replaced by something else: namely, something that will serve the afore-men-tioned needs. Thus, we take the attitude that the sequestration of water into underground reservoirs needs to be replaced by something else: a well, for instance. But given this, it seems that, if intervening in nature for the sake of art is an aesthetic affront to nature, then so are all of these other things also; indeed, practically everything we do would be an aes-thetic affront to nature, on this reasoning.[22] For in each of these cases, we 'mess with' nature's aesthetic qualities. But it seems absurd to say that drawing water, farming and building houses are aesthetic affronts to nature. To take the notion of an affront this way would be to overreact to the possibility of treating nature unethically, to succumb to a sort of ethical hysteria. Moreover, putting this view into practice in any serious way is completely out of the question, since doing so would rob human-ity of the basic necessities of life. For these reasons, it is argued, we ought to reject the claim that the creation of environmental art is ethically problematic, in the sense of constituting an aesthetic affront to nature.

This response is surely correct in assuming that any line of thought that renders the drawing of water, the building of houses and the growing of food affronts to nature is absurd and unacceptable. Such a view would stretch the concept of affront beyond all recognition. Yet it is not so obvi-ous that taking environmental art to be an affront to nature really entails viewing these other actions as affronts to nature. This is because there is an important difference between environmental art and the other sorts of activities in question: the latter have a clear kind of exigency, a practical necessity for life. A common stricture on ethical obligations is that 'ought implies can': if someone has an ethical obligation to do something, then it must be possible, at least in some reasonable circumstances, for the person to do that thing. We could blame a man for failing to rescue an infant from a collapsing building, if he had the time to seize it. But it would be inane to blame him for failing to hold up the collapsing building. This is because it is not physically possible for a human being to hold up a collapsing building. Likewise, there are no reasonable circumstances in which we can forego 'messing with' nature's aesthetic qualities by drawing water or growing food. Since ought implies can, we cannot fault someone for messing with nature's aesthetic qualities in these ways.

But in the case of environmental art, this line of defence is not readily available, in the way that it is available for drawing water, building homes and growing food. For there is, apparently, no parallel practical necessity to create environmental artworks from nature: here the 'messing with nature' is gratuitous, and therefore, open to ethical evaluation. To show that creating environmental art is really like drawing water or growing food, the defender of environmental art must argue that there actually is a practical necessity to create such works. This brings us to a very large philosophical issue – the value of, and need for, art in general – but we can at least note here the difficulty involved in this task. Artists often speak of the necessity of their art, in the sense that they feel compelled to create it. Some force inside them, they say, impels them to do what they do. But this is not the sort of necessity required to deflect the charge of effrontery, for it is not a practical necessity. Generally speaking, no one will die or suffer pain without environmental artworks. No one would deny that, in general, environmental artworks might make life more pleasant or interesting, but it is simply not practically necessary that such artworks be created, in the way that it is necessary for us to draw water and build homes. If the creation of environmental art is to be excused from ethical evaluation, it must be shown that these works not only make human life more pleasant or interesting, but that they contribute to human life in some deep, essential way. The case must be made that without them, human life would be radically impoverished. Whether such a case can be made is an interesting question, but one that we must forgo, for to pursue it would take us entirely into the philosophy of art, and so at last beyond the subject of aesthetics and nature.

NOTES

CHAPTER 1

1 For information on these Areas of Outstanding Natural Beauty, see www.countryside.gov.uk/LAR/Landscape/DL/aonbs/index.asp

2 A view along these lines is developed in McKibben (1989). For critical discussion of this conception of nature, see also Cronon (1995) and Callicott (1998).

3 Mill (1958: 6); for a related view, see Budd (2002: 3–4).

4 Both examples are from Ross (2006: see especially section 7).

5 Destroying nature in this sense would require that humans destroy the entire universe, or come to cause *all* of the events that occur in some reasonably large chunk of it. The latter, even if it is logically possible, seems thankfully beyond the realm of practical feasibility. Worries about destroying the entire universe, on the other hand, do occasionally surface in the particle physics community; see, e.g. Browne (1999). None of this is to say that humanity cannot irrevocably wreck the planet. But destroying nature, in Mill's sense, is not necessary for this.

6 In what follows, we will employ Mill's broader definition of 'nature'.

7 Knight (1808: 9); see also Collingwood (1938: 38).

8 Knight (1808: 9).

9 Collingwood (1938: 39).

10 These are long entrenched usage: the Greek word corresponding to 'beautiful', *kalon*, for example, was commonly used in the former sense; on the history of these usages, see Tatarkiewicz (1972).

11 Tolstoy (1995: 36).

12 Fisher (1998: 172).

13 This definition is due to Tatarkiewicz (1972: 167). The prominence of proportion was supported by Pythagoreanism, an influential strand of Greek thought that took numbers, and their relations, to be the most fundamental features of reality.

14 Plato (1997: 454 [64e]).

15 Tatarkiewicz (1972: 167).

16 On the proportion of the human form, see Vitruvius (1960: Book 3, Chapter 1).

17 Vogel (1998: 16).

18   A paradigm example of a formal garden is that constructed at Versailles for Louis XIV in the seventeenth century. Stephanie Ross describes the basic form of this kind of garden as 'rectilinear and architectural, unified by recurrent geometry and relentless axial symmetry' (1998: 26). Formal gardens, and gardens in general, are discussed further in Chapter 8.

19   Ibid., 34–5; see also Nicolson (1963: 59–62).

20   For a detailed discussion of this view, and its influence, see ibid., Chapter 2.

21   Quoted in ibid., 62.

22   On the resurgence of the Grand Tour, see Ross (1998: 34–40).

23   On the influence of Italian landscape painting on England during this period, see Hussey (1927).

24   Nicolson (1963).

25   John Dixon Hunt (1992: 106) notes John Ruskin's opinion that the vagueness of the expression 'picturesque' was exceeded only by that of phrases from theology. For further discussion of the picturesque, see, in addition to the latter, Ross (1987) and Andrews (1989).

26   These three features were given central importance by Uvedale Price in his *Essay on the Picturesque* (1794).

27   Kant (2000: 144 [section 28]).

28   Quoted in Nicolson (1963: 277).

29   Shaftesbury (1964: 245).

30   See Saito (1985). For a general survey of work on cultural differences in aesthetics, see Higgins (2003).

31   Two attempts to relate the aesthetics of landscapes to evolutionary theory are Appleton (1975) and Orians and Heerwagen (1992). Philosophical perspectives on such efforts are offered by Fisher (2001: 267–8) and Dutton (2003: 697–8).

32   Plato (1965: 4 [287d]).

33   Shaftesbury (1964: 246).

34   This traditional view is well-documented, from a critical perspective, by Korsmeyer (1999: Chapters 1 and 2).

35   Santayana went so far as to define beauty as 'pleasure regarded as the quality of a thing'; see Santayana (1955: 31). Note that Santayana allowed the possibility that *some* pleasures of the proximal senses might be experienced as disembodied, but considered these exceptional cases.

36   For recent overviews of approaches to defining the concept of the aesthetic, see Goldman (2001), Iseminger (2003) and Stecker (2006).

CHAPTER 2

1   The idea of a proposition leads one quickly into many important and complex questions in metaphysics and the philosophy of language, all of which

we will ignore here. For a concise overview of some of the relevant issues, see Loux (2002: Chapter 4).

2   The experience of raw sensations often gives rise to thoughts, of course, and this sometimes tempts us to confuse it with thought. For example, we sometimes speak of people experiencing 'false pains'. A feeling of pain could be said to be false in the sense that it is a psychosomatic pain, one that is purely 'in one's head' and without the usual physical cause. But in this case the feeling of pain itself is not false in the same sense that the proposition 'it rained in Toronto on 26 May 2007' is false. What is false in the former situation is the belief that this pain is caused by a particular bodily problem. This belief does involve a proposition, which is either true or false, depending on whether the pain is caused by this bodily problem or not.

3   Hepburn (1993: 66–7).

4   Ibid., 67; emphasis in original.

5   Brady (1998) and (2003); see also Carroll (2001) and Fudge (2001).

6   Thompson (1995).

7   Wordsworth (1967c).

8   Sagoff (1974: 243).

9   Carlson (2000: Chapter 14); for some related examples see Heyd (2001).

10 Brady (1998: 143).

11 Hepburn (1966: 57); the cloud example is from Carroll (2001: 391).

12 This example is due to Ned Hettinger.

13 Callisto's fate is recounted in book one of Ovid (1986).

14 Hepburn frames the issue yet more generally, as one of the applicability of dichotomies like truth/falsity, depth/shallowness and profundity/triviality to the aesthetic appreciation of nature (1966: 43).

15 Croce (1922: 99).

16 Ibid.

17 Ibid., 99–100.

18 The label and the analogy are proposed by Carlson (2000: 9–10).

19 Views along these lines can be found in Santayana (1955) and Walton (1970).

20 Heyd (2001).

21 Hepburn (1993: 71).

22 Shelley (1967); Wordsworth (1967a).

23 Hepburn (1993: 74).

24 The following example is adapted from Borges' well-known story 'Pierre Menard, Author of the *Quixote*' (1964).

25 Walton (1970). This is not to say that people ought never to employ these ways of thinking of the artworks, but only that they do not carry weight in critical assessments.

26 The position that it cannot is developed and defended by Carlson (2000: Chapter 5).

27 For an argument that humans and some non-human animals are sufficiently similar, see Singer (1990).

28 Carlson (2000: Chapter 5).

29 Hepburn (1966: 45).

30 On the notion of respect for nature in relation to aesthetics, see Hepburn (1993) and (1998: 271) and Saito (1998b), as well as Eaton (1998) and Fudge (2001).

31 Saito (1998b: 136).

32 Taylor (1986).

33 See ibid., Chapter 4.

34 Note that both opponents and proponents of the human consumption of animals for food regard themselves as open to the 'true nature' of animals: see Singer (1990) and Rolston (1991).

35 See Carlson (2000: 66–8).

36 Eaton (1998: 152–3).

37 Sagoff (1974: 228).

CHAPTER 3

1 Formalism can also be developed in terms of auditory perceptual experiences, although for simplicity's sake we will focus upon visual experiences in this chapter. For further discussion of the aesthetics of natural sounds, see Fisher (1998) and (1999).

2 Bell (1913: 8).

3 Ibid., 27.

4 Ibid., 53.

5 Ibid., 13.

6 On the indeterminateness of nature as an object of aesthetic appreciation, see Santayana (1955: 83–4) and Budd (2002).

7 Carlson (2000: 32–3).

8 Knight (1808); for a discussion of Knight's view of the picturesque, see Ross (1987).

9 Ibid., 271.

10 On these devices, see Maillet (2004).

11 Gilpin discusses such use of the Claude mirror (1834: volume II, 233–5).

12 West (1789: 12).

13 Crawford (2004: 259).

14 Bell (1913: 25).

15 Zangwill (2001: 224).

16 Stecker (1997: 396).

17 Kenneth Clark, for example, claims that the curves of a horse's body are 'without question the most satisfying piece of formal relationship in nature' (1977: 36).

18 Daniel (2001: 271).

19 Ibid., 272; emphasis in original. For an overview of similar approaches, see Carlson (1998).

20 Danto (1981: 1–3).

21 Ibid., 1.

22 'Duchamp's urinal tops art survey', BBC News (http://news.bbc.co.uk/2/hi/entertainment/4059997.stm).

23 The example is adapted from Walton (1970: 345); see also Carlson (2000: Chapter 2).

24 Hepburn (1993: 73). This line of argument is developed at length in Carlson (2000: Chapter 3).

25 Hepburn (1993: 73).

26 Berleant (1992); Carlson (2000: 34–5).

27 Callicott (2003a: 137).

28 Carlson (1977).

CHAPTER 4

1 For a detailed development and defence of the science-based approach, see Carlson (2000); a shorter presentation is Carlson (2007).

2 The Milky Way example is discussed by Budd (2002: 21).

3 Carlson (2000: 50).

4 Ibid.

5 Ibid.

6 Leopold (1966: 179).

7 Carlson (2000: 55).

8 Peter Benchley's novel *Jaws* (1974), along with Stephen Spielberg's 1975 film adaptation, did much to popularize the image of the Great White Shark as a mindless human-eating machine. Towards the end of his life, however, Benchley became a public advocate for the protection of sharks, and attempted to counter his own portrait of the Great White, which he believed had been scientifically refuted; see Brown and Mackie (2000).

9 Eaton (1998: 177).

10 Evernden (1983: 3).

11 Leopold (1966: 180).

12 Rolston (2000: 584).

13 Saito (1998b: 143).

14 I take this example from ibid., 131; the quotation is from Hornaday's letter to John K. Small, 30 December 1932, cited in Runte (1979: 131).
15 Evernden (1983: 3).
16 Ibid.
17 Leopold (1966: 180).
18 According to some estimates, certain parts of the prairie are more species rich than the rain forests of California or the Florida everglades; see Savage (2004: 28–9).
19 Ibid., 8.
20 Hepburn (1966).
21 Callicott (2003b: 42).
22 *Cf.* Danto's red square exhibition, discussed in Chapter 3.
23 Saito (1998a: 105).
24 Carlson (2000: 93).
25 Ross (2005: 252); emphasis added.
26 Brady (2003: 99).
27 Heyd (2001).
28 Wordsworth (1967b).
29 Twain (1984: 96); Twain's response is discussed by Saito (1998b: 144) and Carlson (2000: Chapter 2).
30 Heyd (2001: 128–9).
31 Hepburn (1993: 71).
32 Saito (1998b: 144–5). For a different approach, see Parsons (2002).
33 Hettinger (2008: 431).
34 Botkin (1990).
35 Parsons (2006).
36 Budd (2002: 102).
37 Diffey (1993: 48).

CHAPTER 5

1 The label 'pluralism' is due to Carlson (2000: 10).
2 Crawford (2004: 261); *cf.* Stecker (1997).
3 Newman (2001: section 1).
4 Carroll (1993: 245).
5 Ibid., 250.
6 Carroll (2001: 393).
7 Carroll (1993: 251).
8 Ibid., 262 and 245.
9 Carroll (1993: 253).
10 Carroll (2001: 252).

11   Saito (1998a: 102).
12   Saito (1998b: 147).
13   Ibid.
14   Hepburn (1998: 272).
15   See ibid., but also Hepburn (1993).
16   Ibid., 69.
17   Recent overviews of this issue are Gaut (2001) and Kieran (2003).
18   Carroll (1993: 260).
19   See Parsons and Carlson (2004).
20   Carroll (1993: 260).

CHAPTER 6

1   See, for example, the formalist approaches described in Chapter 3, section 1.
2   Berleant (1991: 27).
3   *Atman* is installed at the Cincinnati Art Museum.
4   Berleant (1964: 187).
5   Ibid., 189.
6   Berleant (1991: 28).
7   Ibid., 29.
8   Ibid., 45.
9   Ibid., 46.
10   Berleant (1992: 170).
11   Ibid. 167–71.
12   Burke (1968: 58 [part II, section 2]).
13   Kant (2000: 144–5 [section 28]).
14   Foster (1998: 133).
15   Ibid., 132–3.
16   Ibid., 133.
17   Ibid., 134.
18   Ibid.
19   Ibid., 128.
20   Ibid., 133.
21   Foster is aware of this problem, but offers little in the way of a solution.
22   Berleant (1991: 28).
23   This criticism is developed in Carlson (1993).
24   In addition to the works by Berleant cited above, see Shusterman (2006).
25   At times, Berleant suggests that what is definitive of the aesthetic is not engagement *per se*, but 'the intrinsic perception of sensation', which engagement facilitates (1964: 186). By this Berleant seems to mean that an

experience is aesthetic if we focus only on the qualities of sensations that are given immediately to us: for example, the intensity of a sensation of exertion, or the sharpness of a pain. But, as pointed out in Chapter 1, this does not seem sufficient for aesthetic experience either: the man in a warm bath who reflects only on the qualities of the suffusing warmth that he feels is not thereby having an aesthetic experience, but merely a pleasant one.

CHAPTER 7

1   The distinction between conservation and preservation is drawn by Passmore (1974: 73).
2   Leopold (1966: 262).
3   Rolston (2002: 140). On the role of aesthetic value in Rolston's environmental ethics, see Carlson (2006).
4   Carlson (2000: Chapter 9).
5   Sober (1986).
6   Rolston (2002: 127).
7   This case is described in detail in Brady (2003: Chapter 8).
8   Ibid., 239.
9   This case is described in detail by Lee (1995).
10 Quoted in ibid., 214.
11 For general information on the refuge, see the U.S. government's official website at http://arctic.fws.gov.
12 See Chapter 4, section 2.
13 Steven's remarks were aired on the PSB News Hour, 2 November 2005 (video of his speech is available online at www.pbs.org/newshour/bb/environment/july-dec05/anwr_11–2.html). Some other statements along these lines are quoted in Loftis (2003: 49, n. 13).
14 Of course, people sometimes do come to value physical currency for itself (i.e. intrinsically). Coin collectors do this with old money, and regular folks sometimes develop nostalgic or sentimental attachments to their national currency, particularly when it is threatened with elimination. But the typical value that people accord to currency is merely instrumental value.
15 See Chapter 3. Consider, for instance, Zangwill's remark on the polar bear: 'Need one consider the underwater-swimming polar bear as a beautiful *living* thing or a beautiful *natural* thing or just as a beautiful *thing*? I think this last will do. It is a formally extraordinary *phenomenon*' (2001: 214).
16 Routley and Routley (1980: 137).
17 See Sober (1986: 189) and Thompson (1995: 294).
18 For a brief survey, see Elliot (2001).
19 For arguments along these lines, see Sober (1986) and Thompson (1995).

20 The example is adapted from Godlovitch (1989: 175).

21 See ibid., and Lee (1995).

22 On this issue, see also the discussion of quantification in Chapter 3, sections 2 and 3.

23 Loftis (2003: 43).

24 Ibid.

25 Sober (1986: 194).

26 Hettinger offers the hypothetical example of 'building the Sistine Chapel in some aesthetically undistinguished natural area' (2005: 64).

27 This example, which involved Hetch Hetchy valley in Yosemite National Park, is discussed by Saito (1998b: 146).

28 The classic account of camp is Sontag (1969); it is applied to the context of aesthetically appreciating the environment by Carlson (2000: Chapter 9).

29 Saito (1984: 42).

30 The work of photographer Edward Burtynsky powerfully demonstrates the potential aesthetic value of industrial landscapes; see Pauli (2003).

31 Hettinger (2005: 72).

32 Thompson (1995).

33 Ibid., 304.

34 Ibid.

35 Hettinger (2005: 75).

36 Saito (1984: 45).

37 Hettinger (2005: 75).

CHAPTER 8

1 Ross says that nineteenth-century advances in indoor seedling propagation 'allowed gardeners to trump nature', and 'severed connections between gardens and the natural world' (1999: 13).

2 On the fascinating history of the tulip, see Pavord (1999).

3 On this division, see Miller (1993: 22–3) and Ross (1998: Chapter 2).

4 Ibid., 26.

5 Miller (1993: 77–8).

6 Budd (2002: 8–9).

7 Ross (1998: xii).

8 Ibid., Chapter 3. On these gardens, and their relationship to the arts, see also Hunt (1992).

9 Ross (1998: 202); Miller argues that certain features of gardens make them generally unsuitable for use as an artistic medium (1993: Chapter 4), but for counter-arguments see Leddy (1988).

10 Miller draws a similar distinction between humble and grand gardens (1993: 21). Ross (2006: section 11) describes any garden that is not an Artwork as a 'vernacular' garden, but this term ill befits large scale, professionally designed gardens that fall short of Art status (the Victorian-era Public Gardens in Halifax, Nova Scotia, for example, or the Butchart Gardens in Victoria, British Columbia).

11 Crichton (1991).

12 The scientists in the novel use recovered natural DNA for their dinosaur creation project, but this is not essential: since DNA can be manufactured synthetically, any functional coding sequence could be employed.

13 Ross (2006: section 11).

14 Miller (1993: 15).

15 Indeed, it is not clear that, in stating her definition, Miller is using 'natural' in our sense; thus it is not clear what her considered view of the issue would be.

16 *Cf.* the wilderness experience machine of Routley and Routley (1980), discussed in Chapter 7.

17 Wilson (1984: 114).

18 On the 'no grow' garden trend, see Fletcher (2006).

19 For discussion, see Ross (1998: 206–7); pictures of the Davis garden, and the 'trellis garden' mentioned below, are included as colour plates six and seven in Ross's book.

20 Ibid., 203–4.

21 On this distinction, see Miller (1993: 10).

22 Both Ross and Miller reject this idea, citing Zen gardens as counterexamples; see Ross (1999: 5) and Miller (1993: 9–10). It is true that such gardens, the famous Ryoanji gardens at Kyoto, for example, contain little living material. But while entities of this type are clearly gardens in the 'area adjacent to a building' sense, it is not clear that they are gardens in the gardening sense. When the caretakers of the Ryoanji garden repair its walls, what they are doing does not seem to be the sort of activity we call 'gardening'.

23 Wilson (1984: 115).

24 Wilson is objecting to the general trend towards replacing living things with non-living artefacts.

25 Kant (2000: 179 [section 42]).

26 Ibid.

27 The relevant question here is: would we take an immediate interest in this beauty if the birds and flowers were alive, but yet artificial?

CHAPTER 9

1 In this chapter, we will use the word 'art' to refer to what we called 'Art' in the last chapter: that is, something that is created by people who describe

themselves as 'artists', shown in galleries, critiqued by art critics, and
so on.

2   See Kimmelman (2002).

3   Carlson (2000: 150).

4   The rider 'in some substantial sense' is needed in order to differentiate
environmental art from artworks that employ nature only as an ultimate
source of materials. Thus landscape paintings do not count as environmental art even if some of the materials used in manufacturing paints are natural
materials.

5   The general idea of an aesthetic affront was first articulated by Donald
Crawford (1983); Allen Carlson endorses and further develops it his (2000:
Chapter 10).

6   Ibid., 154.

7   Ibid., 155.

8   Ibid., 154.

9   An actual artwork that is interesting to consider in this context is Robert
Rauschenberg's *Erased de Kooning* (1953), which he created by erasing a
drawing by the artist William de Kooning.

10   Ibid., 156.

11   As mentioned, Goldsworthy's works are often transient; another environmental artist known for ephemeral works is Christo.

12   This is the general approach of three recent reconsiderations of environmental art: Brady (2007), Brook (2007) and Lintott (2007).

13   Brady says that the charge of effrontery is justified in the case of *Double
Negative* (2007: 290).

14   Ibid., 289.

15   Ibid., 292.

16   Brady quotes the phrase 'macho aggression' from Malcolm Andrews (1999:
213).

17   Carlson is dismissive of the notion that environmental art can aesthetically
improve nature, arguing that, in fact, 'virgin nature by and large has positive
aesthetic qualities' and that 'none of virgin nature is comparable to the work
of a third-rate hack' (2000: 157). As we have seen in Chapter 7, however,
even if Positive Aesthetics is true, it is implausible to think that nature can
never be improved aesthetically through human intervention.

18   The importance of aesthetic improvement comes out clearly in Brook
(2007), who considers the case of the recent construction of an underwater
gnome garden by divers in Wastwater Park. Though not an artwork, this
'work' certainly has aesthetic qualities, which Brook describes compel-
lingly: an absurd appearance, an 'organic feel', an expressiveness of daring
and defiance, and so on. Although she does not explicitly appeal to these
aesthetic features as grounds for justifying such 'aesthetic interventions'

in nature, the drift of her discussion is that there is something new and aesthetically valuable in 'works' of this kind.

19 Heyd suggests that even intrusive earthworks, such as *Double Negative*, may serve this function, since they 'leave the onlooker no choice but to reflect on the place of human intervention in wild nature and, in this way, may lead to renewed attention to the supposedly justified intervention of the everyday' (2002).

20 Lintott (2007: 276).

21 Humphrey (1985: 19–20).

22 This idea is discussed by Godlovitch (1998).

BIBLIOGRAPHY

Andrews, M. (1989), *The Search for the Picturesque* (Stanford: Stanford University Press).

— (1999), *Landscape and Western Art* (New York: Oxford University Press).

Appleton, J. (1975), *The Experience of Landscape* (New York: John Wiley & Sons).

Bell, C. (1913), *Art* (New York: Frederick A. Stokes).

Berleant, A. (1964), 'The Sensuous and the Sensual in Aesthetics', *Journal of Aesthetics and Art Criticism*, 23, 185–92.

— (1991), *Art and Engagement* (Philadelphia: Temple University Press).

— (1992), 'The Aesthetics of Art and Nature', in *The Aesthetics of Environment* (Philadelphia: Temple University Press).

Borges, J.L. (1964), 'Pierre Menard, Author of the *Quixote*', in D.A. Yates and J.E. Irby (eds), *Labyrinths: Selected Stories & Other Writings* (New York: New Directions Publishing), 36–44.

Botkin, D. (1990), *Discordant Harmonies: A New Ecology for the Twenty-First Century* (Oxford: Oxford University Press).

Brady, E. (1998), 'Imagination and the Aesthetic Appreciation of Nature', *Journal of Aesthetics and Art Criticism*, 56, 139–47.

— (2003), *Aesthetics of the Natural Environment* (Edinburgh and Tuscaloosa: Edinburgh University Press and University of Alabama Press).

— (2007), 'Aesthetic Regard for Nature in Environmental and Land Art', *Ethics, Place & Environment*, 10, 287–300.

Brook, I. (2007), Aesthetic Aspects of Unauthorised Environmental Interventions', *Ethics, Place & Environment*, 10, 307–18.

Brown, P. and D. Mackie (2000), '*Jaws* Author Campaigns to Save the Shark', *The Guardian*, 7 July.

Browne, M. (1999), 'Will Brookhaven Destroy the Universe? Probably Not', *New York Times*, 10 August.

Budd, M. (2002), *The Aesthetic Appreciation of Nature: Essays on the Aesthetics of Nature* (Oxford: Oxford University Press).

Burke, E. (1968) [1757], *A Philosophical Enquiry into the Origin of Our Ideas of the Sublime and Beautiful*, J.T. Boulton (ed.) (Notre Dame, IN: University of Notre Dame Press).

Callicott, J.B. (1998), 'The Wilderness Idea Revisited: The Sustainable Development Alternative', in J.B. Callicott and M.P. Nelson (eds), *The Great New Wilderness Debate* (Athens: University of Georgia Press), 337–66.

— (2003a), 'The Land Aesthetic', in S.J. Armstrong and R.G. Botzler (eds), *Environmental Ethics: Divergence & Convergence* (third edn) (New York: McGraw-Hill), 135–43.

— (2003b), 'Wetland Gloom and Wetland Glory', *Philosophy and Geography*, 6, 33–45.

Carlson, A. (1977), 'On the Possibility of Quantifying Scenic Beauty', *Landscape Planning*, 4, 131–72.

— (1993), 'Aesthetics and Engagement', *British Journal of Aesthetics*, 33, 220–7.

— (1998), 'Landscape Assessment', in M. Kelly (ed.), *Encyclopedia of Aesthetics* (New York: Oxford University Press), vol. 3, 102–5.

— (2000), *Aesthetics and the Environment: The Appreciation of Nature, Art and Architecture* (London: Routledge).

— (2006), '"We See Beauty Now Where We Could Not See It Before": Rolston's Aesthetics of Nature', in C. Preston and W. Ouderkirk (eds), *Nature, Value, Duty: Life on Earth with Holmes Rolston III* (Dordrecht: Springer), 103–24.

— (2007), 'The Requirements for an Adequate Aesthetics of Nature', *Environmental Philosophy*, 4, 1–12.

Carroll, N. (1993), 'On Being Moved by Nature: Between Religion and Natural History', in S. Kemal and I. Gaskel (eds), *Landscape, Natural Beauty and the Arts* (Cambridge: Cambridge University Press), 244–66.

— (2001), 'Emotion, Appreciation, and Nature', in *Beyond Aesthetics: Philosophical Essays* (New York: Cambridge University Press), 384–94.

Clark, K. (1977), *Animals and Men: The Relationship as Reflected in Western Art from Prehistory to the Present Day* (New York: William Morrow and Company).

Collingwood, R.G. (1938), *The Principles of Art* (Oxford: Oxford University Press).

Crawford, D. (1983), 'Art and Nature: Some Dialectical Relationships', *Journal of Aesthetics and Art Criticism*, 42, 49–58.

— (2004), 'Scenery and the Aesthetics of Nature', in A. Carlson and A. Berleant (eds), *The Aesthetics of Natural Environments* (Peterborough, ON: Broadview Press), 253–68.

Crichton, M. (1991), *Jurassic Park* (New York: Ballantine Books).

Croce, B. (1922) [1909], *Aesthetic as Science of Expression and General Linguistic*, D. Ainslie (trans.) (New York: Noonday Press).

Cronon, W. (1995), 'The Trouble with Wilderness; or, Getting Back to the Wrong Nature', in W. Cronon (ed.), *Uncommon Ground: Rethinking the Human Place in Nature* (New York: W.W. Norton & Company), 69–90.

Daniel, T.C. (2001), 'Whither Scenic Beauty? Visual Landscape Quality Assessment in the 21st Century', *Landscape and Urban Planning*, 54, 267–81.

Danto, A. (1981), *The Transfiguration of the Commonplace: A Philosophy of Art* (Cambridge, MA: Harvard University Press).

Diffey, T. (1993), 'Natural Beauty without Metaphysics', in S. Kemal and I. Gaskel (eds), *Landscape, Natural Beauty and the Arts* (Cambridge: Cambridge University Press), 43–64.

Dutton, D. (2003), 'Aesthetics and Evolutionary Psychology', in J. Levinson (ed.), *Oxford Handbook of Aesthetics* (Oxford: Oxford University Press), 693–705.

Eaton, M. (1998), 'Fact and Fiction in the Aesthetic Appreciation of Nature', *Journal of Aesthetics and Art Criticism*, 56, 149–56.

Elliot, R. (2001), 'Normative Ethics', in D. Jamieson (ed.), *A Companion to Environmental Philosophy* (Oxford: Blackwell), 177–91.

Evernden, N. (1983), 'Beauty and Nothingness: Prairie as Failed Resource', *Landscape Magazine*, 27, 1–8.

Fisher, J.A. (1998), 'What the Hills Are Alive With: In Defense of the Sounds of Nature', *Journal of Aesthetics and Art Criticism*, 56, 167–79.

— (1999), 'The Value of Natural Sounds', *The Journal of Aesthetic Education*, 33, 26–42.

— (2001), 'Aesthetics', in D. Jamieson (ed.), *A Companion to Environmental Philosophy* (Oxford: Blackwell), 264–76.

Fletcher, J. (2006), 'The Concrete Gardener', *Wall Street Journal Online*, 29 September.

Foster, C. (1998), 'The Narrative and the Ambient in Environmental Aesthetics', *Journal of Aesthetics and Art Criticism*, 56, 127–37.

Fudge, R. (2001), 'Imagination and the Science-Based Aesthetic Appreciation of Unscenic Nature', *Journal of Aesthetics and Art Criticism*, 59, 275–88.

Gaut, B. (2001), 'Art and Ethics', in B. Gaut and D.M. Lopes (eds), *The Routledge Companion to Aesthetics* (London: Routledge), 341–52.

Gilpin, W. (1834) [1791], *Remarks on Forest Scenery, and Other Woodland Views* (London: Smith, Elder & Co.).

Godlovitch, S. (1989), 'Aesthetic Protectionism', *Journal of Applied Philosophy*, 6, 171–80.

— (1998), 'Offending Against Nature', *Environmental Values*, 7, 131–50.

Goldman, A. (2001), 'The Aesthetic', in B. Gaut and D.M. Lopes (eds), *The Routledge Companion to Aesthetics* (London: Routledge), 181–92.

Hargrove, E. (1989), *Foundations of Environmental Ethics* (Englewood Cliffs, NJ: Prentice Hall).

Hepburn, R. (1966), 'Contemporary Aesthetics and the Neglect of Natural Beauty', in B. Williams and A. Montefiore (eds), *British Analytical Philosophy* (London: Routledge and Kegan Paul), 285–310.

— (1993), 'Trivial and Serious in Aesthetic Appreciation of Nature', in S. Kemal and I. Gaskel (eds), *Landscape, Natural Beauty and the Arts* (Cambridge: Cambridge University Press), 65–80.

— (1998), 'Nature Humanised: Nature Respected,' *Environmental Values*, 7, 267–79.

Hettinger, N. (2005), 'Allen Carlson's Environmental Aesthetics and Protection of the Environment', *Environmental Ethics*, 27, 57–76.

— (2008), 'Objectivity in Environmental Aesthetics and Environmental Protection', in A. Carlson and S. Lintott (eds), *Nature, Aesthetics, and Environmentalism: From Beauty to Duty* (New York: Columbia University Press), 413–37.

Heyd, T. (2001), 'Aesthetic Appreciation and the Many Stories about Nature', *British Journal of Aesthetics*, 4, 125–37.

— (2002), 'Nature Restoration without Dissimulation: Learning from Japanese Gardens and Earthworks', *Essays in Philosophy*, 2 (www.humboldt.edu/~essays).

Higgins, K. (2003), 'Comparative Aesthetics', in J. Levinson (ed.), *Oxford Handbook of Aesthetics* (Oxford: Oxford University Press), 679–92.

Humphrey, P. (1985), 'The Ethics of Earthworks', *Environmental Ethics*, 7, 5–21.

Hunt, J.D. (1992), *Gardens and the Picturesque: Studies in the History of Landscape Architecture* (Cambridge, MA: MIT Press).

Hussey, C. (1927), *The Picturesque: Studies in a Point of View* (London: G.P. Putnam's Sons).

Iseminger, G. (2003), 'Aesthetic Experience', in J. Levinson (ed.), *Oxford Handbook of Aesthetics* (Oxford: Oxford University Press), 99–116.

Kant, I. (2000) [1790], *Critique of the Power of Judgment*, P. Guyer and E. Matthews (trans.) (Cambridge: Cambridge University Press).

Kieran, M. (2003), 'Art and Morality', in J. Levinson (ed.), *Oxford Handbook of Aesthetics* (Oxford: Oxford University Press), 451–70.

Kimmelman, M. (2002), 'Out of the Deep', *New York Times*, 13 October.

Knight, R. (1808) [1805], *An Analytical Inquiry into the Principles of Taste* (fourth edn) (London: Payne and White).

Korsmeyer, C. (1999), *Making Sense of Taste: Food and Philosophy* (Ithaca: Cornell University Press).

Leddy, T. (1988), 'Gardens in an Expanded Field', *British Journal of Aesthetics*, 28, 327–40.

Lee, K. (1995), 'Beauty for Ever?', *Environmental Values*, 4, 213–25.

Leopold, A. (1966), *A Sand County Almanac, with Essays on Conservation from Round River* (New York: Ballantine Books).

Lintott, S. (2007), 'Ethically Evaluating Land Art: Is It Worth It?', *Ethics, Place & Environment*, 10, 263–77.

Loftis, R.J. (2003), 'Three Problems for the Aesthetic Foundations of Environmental Ethics', *Philosophy in the Contemporary World*, 10, 41–50.

Loux, M.J. (2002), *Metaphysics: A Contemporary Introduction* (second edn) (London: Routledge).

Maillet, A. (2004), *The Claude Glass: Use and Meaning of the Black Mirror in Western Art*, J. Fort (trans.) (New York: Zone Books).

McKibben, B. (1989), *The End of Nature* (New York: Random House).

Mill, J.S. (1958) [1874], 'Nature', in *Nature and Utility of Religion*, G. Nakhnikian (ed.) (New York: Liberal Arts Press).

Miller, M. (1993), *The Garden as an Art* (Albany, NY: State University of New York Press).

Newman, I. (2001), 'Reflections on Allen Carlson's *Aesthetics and the Environment*', *AE: Canadian Aesthetics Journal*, 6 (www.uqtr.uquebec.ca/AE/Vol_6/Carlson/newman.html).

Nicolson, M.H. (1963), *Mountain Gloom and Mountain Glory: The Development of the Aesthetics of the Infinite* (New York: W.W. Norton & Company).

Orians, G.H. and J.H. Heerwagen. (1992), 'Evolved Responses to Landscapes', in J.H. Barkow, L. Cosmides and J. Tooby (eds), *The Adapted Mind: Evolutionary Psychology and the Generation of Culture* (New York: Oxford University Press), 555–79.

Ovid. (1986), *Metamorphoses*, A.D. Melville (trans.) (Oxford: Oxford University Press).

Parsons, G. (2002), 'Nature Appreciation, Science and Positive Aesthetics', *British Journal of Aesthetics*, 42, 279–95.

— (2006), 'Theory, Observation, and the Role of Scientific Understanding in the Aesthetic Appreciation of Nature', *Canadian Journal of Philosophy*, 36, 165–86.

Parsons, G. and A. Carlson. (2004), 'New Formalism and the Aesthetic Appreciation of Nature', *Journal of Aesthetics and Art Criticism*, 62, 363–76.

Passmore, J. (1974), *Man's Responsibility for Nature: Ecological Problems and Western Traditions* (New York: Charles Scribner's Sons).

Pauli, L. (2003), *Manufactured Landscapes: The Photographs of Edward Burtynsky* (Ottawa: National Gallery of Canada and Yale University Press).

Pavord, A. (1999), *The Tulip* (New York: Bloomsbury).

Plato. (1965), 'Greater Hippias', B. Jowett (trans.), in K. Aschenbrenner and A. Isenberg (eds), *Aesthetic Theories: Studies in the Philosophy of Art* (Englewood Cliffs, NJ: Prentice Hall), 3–17.

— (1997), *Complete Works*, J.M. Cooper and D.S. Hutchinson (eds), (Indianapolis, IN: Hackett).

Price, U. (1794), *Essay on the Picturesque as Compared with the Sublime and the Beautiful*.

Rolston, H. (1991), 'Challenges in Environmental Ethics', in F.H. Bormann and S.R. Kellert (eds), *Environmental Ethics: Values in and Duties to the Natural World* (New Haven and London: Yale University Press), 73–96.

— (2000), 'Aesthetics in the Swamps', *Perspectives in Biology and Medicine*, 43, 584–97.

— (2002), 'From Beauty to Duty: Aesthetics of Nature and Environmental Ethics', in A. Berleant (ed.), *Environment and the Arts: Perspective on Environmental Aesthetics* (Aldershot: Ashgate), 127–41.

Ross, S. (1987), 'The Picturesque: An Eighteenth-Century Debate', *Journal of Aesthetics and Art Criticism*, 46, 271–9.

— (1998), *What Gardens Mean* (Chicago: University of Chicago Press).

— (1999), 'Gardens' Powers', *Journal of Aesthetic Education*, 33, 4–17.

— (2005), 'Landscape Perception: Theory-Laden, Emotionally Resonant, Politically Correct', *Environmental Ethics*, 27, 245–63.

— (2006), 'Paradoxes and Puzzles: Appreciating Gardens and Urban Nature', *Contemporary Aesthetics*, 4.

Routley, R. and V. Routley. (1980), 'Human Chauvinism and Environmental Ethics', in D.S. Mannison, M.A. McRobbie and R. Routley (eds), *Environmental Philosophy* (Canberra: Department of Philosophy, Australian National University), 96–189.

Runte, A. (1979), *National Parks: The American Experience* (Lincoln, NE: University of Nebraska Press).

Sagoff, M. (1974), 'On Preserving the Natural Environment', *Yale Law Journal*, 84, 205–67.

Saito, Y. (1984), 'Is There a Correct Aesthetic Appreciation of Nature?', *Journal of Aesthetic Education*, 18, 35–46.

— (1985), 'The Japanese Appreciation of Nature', *British Journal of Aesthetics*, 25, 239–51.

— (1998a), 'The Aesthetics of Unscenic Nature', *Journal of Aesthetics and Art Criticism*, 56, 101–11.

— (1998b), 'Appreciating Nature on Its Own Terms', *Environmental Ethics*, 20, 135–49.

Santayana, G. (1955) [1896], *The Sense of Beauty: Being the Outline of Aesthetic Theory* (New York: Dover).

Savage, C. (2004), *Prairie: A Natural History* (Vancouver: Greystone Books).

Shaftesbury, Earl of (A.A. Cooper). (1964) [1711], *Characteristics of Men, Manners, Opinions, Times*, in A. Hofstadter and R. Kuhns (eds), *Philosophies of Art and Beauty: Selected Readings in Aesthetics from Plato to Heidegger* (New York: Modern Library), 241–76.

Shelley, P. (1967) [1817], 'Mont Blanc: Lines Written in the Vale of Chamouni', in D. Perkins (ed.), *English Romantic Writers* (San Diego: Harcourt Brace Jovanovich), 968–70.

Shusterman, R. (2006), 'Aesthetic Experience: From Analysis to Eros', *Journal of Aesthetics and Art Criticism*, 64, 217–30.

Singer, P. (1990), *Animal Liberation* (second edn) (New York: Avon Books).

Sober, E. (1986), 'Philosophical Problems for Environmentalism', in B.G. Norton (ed.), *The Preservation of Species: The Value of Biological Diversity* (Princeton: Princeton University Press), 173–94.

Sontag, S. (1969), 'Notes on "Camp"', in *Against Interpretation* (New York: Dell).

Stecker, R. (1997), 'The Correct and the Appropriate in the Appreciation of Nature', *British Journal of Aesthetics*, 37, 393–402.

— (2006), 'Aesthetic Experience and Aesthetic Value', *Philosophy Compass*, 1, 1–10.

Tatarkiewicz, W. (1972), 'The Great Theory of Beauty and Its Decline', *Journal of Aesthetics and Art Criticism*, 31, 165–80.

Taylor, P. (1986), *Respect for Nature: A Theory of Environmental Ethics* (Princeton: Princeton University Press).

Thompson, J. (1995), 'Aesthetics and the Value of Nature', *Environmental Ethics*, 17, 291–305.

Tolstoy, L. (1995) [1898], *What Is Art?*, R. Pevear and L. Volokhonsky (trans.) (New York: Penguin).

Twain, M. (1984) [1883], *Life on the Mississippi* (New York: Penguin).

Vitruvius. (1960) [1914], *The Ten Books on Architecture*, M.H. Morgan (trans.) (New York: Dover).

Vogel, S. (1998), *Cat's Paws and Catapults: Mechanical Worlds of Nature and People* (New York: W.W. Norton & Company).

Walton, K. (1970), 'Categories of Art', *Philosophical Review*, 68, 334–67.

West, T. (1789) [1778], *A Guide to the Lakes, in Cumberland, Westmorland, and Lancashire* (fourth edn) (London: Richardson, Robson and Pennington).

Wilson, E.O. (1984), *Biophilia* (Cambridge, MA: Harvard University Press).

Wordsworth, W. (1967a) [1798], 'Lines: Composed a Few Miles above Tintern Abbey', in D. Perkins (ed.), *English Romantic Writers* (San Diego: Harcourt Brace Jovanovich), 209–11.

— (1967b) [1798], 'The Tables Turned', in D. Perkins (ed.), *English Romantic Writers* (San Diego: Harcourt Brace Jovanovich), 209.

— (1967c) [1807], 'The World Is Too Much with Us; Late and Soon', in D. Perkins (ed.), *English Romantic Writers* (San Diego: Harcourt Brace Jovanovich), 289.

Zangwill, N. (2001), 'Formal Natural Beauty', *Proceedings of the Aristotelian Society*, 101, 209–24.

INDEX

Adams, A. 40
aesthetic affront
    characterized 130
    see also environmental art
aesthetic incongruity 109
Aesthetic Preservation
    defined 32
    dilemma for 107–13
    and the engaged aesthetic 90–1
    and Formalism 41–3, 47–8
    and Post-modernism 32
    and the science-based view 57–9,
      63–5
    Strong vs. Weak 102–5
aesthetic qualities
    defined 15–7
Alison, A. 35
'analogy with art' argument
    and Formalism 41
    and Moderate Pluralism 70, 79–80
    and Post-modernism 29
    and Robust Pluralism 72–3
    and the science-based view 50–2,
      61–3
Arctic National Wildlife Refuge 97,
    99, 101, 106
artefactualization of nature 104, 115

Bambi 32, 53
'beauty'
    different senses of 4–6
    relation to aesthetic qualities 6–11
Bell, C. 35–7, 40, 83
Berleant, A. 83–94
Blake, W. 61
Brady, E. 22, 96–7
    on environmental art 132
    on the science-based view 60
Brook, I. 133n

Budd, M. 64
Burke, E.
    on the sublime 86–7
Burtynsky, E. 109n

Callicott, J.
    on Formalism 46–7
    on wetlands 56–7
Carlson, A. 22
    on Aesthetic Preservation 96
    on environmental art 131
    on Formalism 46n
    on Positive Aesthetics 58–9, 64–5
    on the science-based view 50–3
Carroll, N.
    on being moved by nature 69–70,
      79–80
Cervantes, M.
    Don Quixote 27, 29
Cézanne, P. 36
Collingwood, R.G. 5
commedia dell'arte 70, 79, 80
Crawford, D. 38, 68
Crichton, M.
    Jurassic Park 121
Croce, B. 24–6, 30, 52, 55

da Vinci, L. 110
    Mona Lisa 131, 134, 137
Daniel, T. 42
Danto, A. 43–4
Davis, C. 123
definition, philosophical 12–5
Delhi Sands flower-loving fly 112
Dennis, J. 10
di Suvero, M.
    Atman 83–4
Diffey, T. 65
disinterestedness 16, 35